digital dreams

digital

dreams

architecture and the new alchemic technologies

neil spiller

●●●ellipsis

● ● ●ellipsis is a registered
trade mark of ellipsis london
limited

cataloguing in publication
a CIP record for this publication
is available from the british
library

first published 1998 by
ellipsis london limited
55 charlotte road
london EC2A 3QT
e-mail ...@ellipsis.co.uk

© neil spiller 1998

laurie farmer worked in
collaboration with neil spiller
on the raw material for the
images on pages 38–39, 54–55,
63, 65, 66, 67, 71, 90, 91, and
115

bob shiel and nick callicott of
sixteen (makers) made the hot
desk (pages 130–135)

edited by annie bridges
colour by shereen rahwangi
design by jonathan moberly

printed in hong kong

ISBN 1 899858 10 5

FOR MELISSA

contents

introduction

Space, the Final Frontier

Beware of the period ahead! Already
this world is cracking, it has within it
some unknown principle of negation,
it is breaking down. Keep an eye on
the rising smoke and the whip applied
by ghosts in the bourgeois world.
Lightning smoulders under the bowler
hats. Mischief is brewing!
    Louis Aragon, *La Peinture au défi*,
1930

Humanity, and consequently architecture, are on the verge of
a major shift in direction. As contemporary technological
explorations into both biological and mechanical systems continue, a reassessment of architectural space is occurring.

Our spacescape is changing. Our flesh and its inert
environment currently imprison us. In the future, this conspiracy will be challenged. Philosophically and ethically we are
in a time of flux. The pseudo-dynamics of architectural
modernism have left us ill-prepared for the physical and spatial changes that are daily rocketing towards us. The potential
difference between now and soon is huge; the shock could be
massive, and many aspects of society will change or die. Yet
many of us still amble about in a naïve reality, convinced of
the *status quo*'s sacrosanct immortality and benevolent good-
ness. This book is about how advanced technologies, such as
cyberspace, molecular and tissue engineering, genetics and the
theories of complex systems, will drastically change our environment – and therefore our architecture. To illustrate the
impact of these technologies, it is necessary to plot some
of the changes that will occur in our spatial lexicon and spec-
ulate on how they will affect our ability to conceive, navigate
and occupy these previously unavailable, technologically
defined landscapes.

Since it is space itself that is being re-evalued, it is
inevitable that this process will lead to a re-articulation of
architecture in terms of its use, effectiveness, scale of operation and aesthetic content. Some will see this as an architectural crisis, others will not see it at all, and still others will see
it as the opening-up of a series of new spatial frontiers. This
book takes the latter approach. The following chapters put
forward a variety of future perspectives that will enable the

disassembling ecstasy......

reader to see the diversity and potential of technological innovation, the interaction of these techniques, and the resultant possible architectures.

Much of the innovative research that is being carried out at the moment is within the general field of 'plectics'. Murray Gell-Mann defines this large branch of science as

… the study of simplicity and complexity. It includes the various attempts to define complexity; the study of the roles of simplicity and complexity and of classical and quantum information in the history of the universe; the physics of information; the study of non-linear dynamics, including chaos theory, strange attractors, and self-similarity in complex non-adaptive systems in physical science; and the study of complex adaptive systems, including prebiotic chemical evolution, biological evolution, the behaviour of individual organisms, the functioning of ecosystems, the operation of mammalian immune systems, learning and thinking, the evolution of human languages, the rise and fall of human cultures, the behaviour of markets, and the operation of computers that are designed or programmed to evolve strategies – say, for playing games or solving problems.[1]

1 See Murray Gell-Mann, 'Plectics', in John Brockman (ed.), *The Third Culture*, Simon and Schuster, 1995.

The search for an holistic theory of science has created many branches of endeavour which have evolved approaches that seek a synthesis between the biological and the mechanical. As this integration continues, the physical and perceptual nature of the human condition will reconfigure. Society will have to reassess what is meant by the 'real' and the 'alive'. With the advent of various surgical and non-surgical procedures, we may even have to change our present concept of death. Architecture cannot continue in its old ways; it must respond to such innovations.

The new architectures will not be without symbolism, but their symbolic language will be a hybrid of established real

digital dreams

● ● ● ● It has often been postulated that society moves relentlessly towards invisibility, a sort of visual and philosophical entropy. The pre-medieval anthropocentric concept of the universe has been superseded by invisible technologies which are no longer linked to the limited dexterity of the human being. As we approach the new millennium, many of the initially more extreme technological theories are coming closer to being realised. Mortality itself is being questioned, and escape from our badly designed, over-hysterical bodies is being proffered. This significant evolutionary fact negates all else: the limits of human form will disappear. All the idiosyncratic architectural items that have honed architectural theory over thousands of years will become mere baubles, to be played with or subsumed into a new hypergeography. The thinking mechanism, with a cultural memory and a combination of inherited, juxtaposed personalities (the cyberspatial cyborg), will be a reflection of different criteria.

symbolism and virtually real symbolism. Architecture as a discipline is ideally suited to the creation of such new mythologies, and it can be shown that architecture itself exhibits many religious traits, including creation mythology and animism. Architecture must become a fulcrum around which the technology that liberates the body and the biology that sustains it are reconciled.

Currently, speculation of this sort is not carried out within the wider architectural community; the cost to architecture of such lack of vision could be its demise. Architecture must become informationally denser. The biomechanical systems of the future will allow an increase in the spatial denseness of architecture. This seems appropriate in a world of ever-increasing info-mass.

The laboratory for this exploration has to encompass the real city, the unreal city, and the visceral and mental spaces of the body – and the blurred spaces in between. The specific issues to be addressed in the light of the re-evaluation of space include algorithmic and hypertextural architectures, shamanistic spatial procedures in cyberspace, self-replicating and artificially intelligent architecture, the alchemic nature of soft and digital spaces, the architectural implications of swarming, hyperstructural biomechanisms, the new plasticity in architecture, and the evolving and split physiology of the human body. These themes are not assessed one by one but are woven together to illustrate various architectural scenarios, as they would be in practice.

During polite dinner parties, when the conversation turns to the future, it is shocking to discover just how uninformed the lay person is concerning the technological advances that are currently contorting space beyond all recognisable limits.

Beyond the Veil of Tears

As a theme for the turn of the millennium, the topic of disappearance seems to be appropriate. But how does one design a logistical happening, or an artefact to reflect this frightening yet liberating fact of the future, using only the dumb tools of today's real world?

This proposal for an urban park, or for a series of interrelated insertions into the 'gap' sites of the city – the urban black holes – is a catalytic gesture, a constant reminder of a 'phase transition' waiting to happen.

Drumlins and Ponds

Perhaps all art needs an initial gratuitous act. With this proposal it was the digging of the amorphous pits. This formal tactic suggested the glacial form of the drumlin as an analogy for the resistance of the thrust of technology and the symbiotic relationship between the shaped and the shaper. Traditional tenets of architectural instigation are of little help when trying to paraphrase 'disappearance' within the context of the contemporary world. Society resists the continuing machinations of science,

As we surround ourselves with superficial symbols of permanency, this ignorance is both understandable and erroneous. *Digital Dreams* attempts to encourage the reader to become more aware of recent scientific theories and concepts. If the reader is an architect it is hoped that the book will act as a catalyst for further speculation about what our future environments will demand or become. The complacency of some within the architectural profession is very dangerous, for the evolving spatial lexicon is uniquely tailored to an expansion of the architect's role. This book acts as both an introduction to some of these spatial opportunities and a source text for areas of research which could fuel further explorations.

Driving on Holy Gasoline

Each chapter is organised as a primary and a secondary text (with notes), interspersed with illustrations and tertiary texts. The conceptual boundary between texts is blurred. As with all knots of knowledge, there is a 'soup' of association that folds in on itself, constantly providing further insight.

Much has been written of the death of God, and of our technologies as the new Hand of Creation. And, indeed, much insight can be gained by using religious analogies when considering recent innovations: many of the new spatial realms can be described in terms of magic, miracles, metamorphosis, resurrection, omnipresence, angels and demons. Strangely, our journeys in the new spacescapes contain all these concepts. From these viewpoints, and a variety of others, this book looks into the future to help the reader to focus on some of the crucial issues that will define some of the architectures that even now are silently but swiftly evolving.

digital dreams

some elements of it more successfully than others. Certain organisations and practices actively conspire against the glacial flow of science and become obstacles. The result of this resistance is mutual attrition, the streamlining of results. In making the park, the initial act – digging the drumlin-shaped pits – transforms the ground surface into a series of cut marks, a space for the penetration, and hence disappearance, of technology into the body of the earth.

Cocoons

Erected on hydraulic pistons are hundreds of cocoons containing the originals or mock-ups of historically and culturally significant objects – Tutankhamen's death mask, the FA Cup, the Turin Shroud. Each cocoon, with its own humidity control, security and so on, is like a museum with one exhibit. These cocoons are then dressed in detritus, the accumulated product of a civilisation about to vanish. The debris will be inorganic scrap.

Into the Pit

The public are encouraged to disassemble, to unravel and to steal, with the cocoons presiding over the spectacle like malevolent deities, each with a prized hostage, mocking man's attempt at rationality. Over a period of time, the audience will return repeatedly to see what else has been revealed and what else can be salvaged. These visitors will witness the gradual and symbolic disappearance of the cocoons into the drumlin-shaped

ponds. Can an academic interest in Tutankhamen compete with the prospect of pilfering a slightly used chrome ashtray? This process sucks the object into submission, steals its uniqueness. The park allows the already vanished another year's visibility – a last encore.

this is the realm of the second

digital dreams

Memory Tears

In the final stage in this eulogy to disappearance, discarded items can be thrown into drumlin-shaped casting pits – collectors of surreal debris. The metal or plastic is then cast in concrete, a contemporary fossil for later analysis. Each drumlin-shaped cast becomes a memorial to the beautiful unforeseen, a strange and surreal clash of form and function. The concrete drumlins are then erected over the ponds. They appear in the park as a series of

unearthly, freeze-frame icons in memory of the act of disappearance – a forest of jagged tears.

When used singularly in 'gap' sites, the concrete tear will become a city marker. Items that have been stolen from the park will be reused – as jewellery or as a subversive element in the home – until they ultimately 'disappear' into it through familiarity. People are just 'wetware' in the program; there is no controllable finished product, only an unpredictable dispersal.

algorithm

The algorithm is the mapping of steps to solve families of problems; providing the initial data input into the sequence is of the correct nature, the process will be completed. For example, an algorithm that adds together two numbers under ten can output a variety of answers if the input is within its range. Therefore, disparate answers are produced according to the values that are input initially. The product cannot be controlled.

aesthetic

This rather simple illustration of a primitive algorithm dislocates the sensitive architectural mind. One aim of this book is to open out technological vistas that result in this type of uncontrollable architectural product.

secrecy and architecture

The purpose of this text is to suggest that architects cannot function without the judicial keeping and telling of secrets, and that this propensity to secrecy is directly linked to the self-replicatory aspirations of the concept of the meme. Memes were first posited by Richard Dawkins, in his book *The Selfish Gene*,[1] as a 'unit of cultural transmission'. Their etymology links them to the Greek *mimeme*, that is, the imitational fragment, memory. Dawkins cites 'tunes, ideas, catch-phrases, clothes, fashion, ways of making pots or building arches' as examples of memes. He theorises that memes have the same replicating aspirations as genes, jumping from meme-nest to meme-nest (mind to mind) in an act of duplication. Further, he suggests that the architectural drawing is the first, and sometimes the only, manifestation of an architectural meme-nest, and therefore of immense archaeological interest. Architects trade memes (some secret, some not) with society. The symbiosis that can exist between architects and memes is characterised by 'the secret'. And sometimes architects choose to reveal this secret to another party for mutual benefit.[2]

1 R Dawkins, *The Selfish Gene*, Oxford University Press, 1976.

Architecture, the most public of arts, can also be the most intensely private. It is an unusual role that architects must fulfil. They must exhibit cultural empathy but at the same time enjoy peripheral thought patterns. It is this need to be at once central yet orbital that forces architects to adopt narratives and notations, some of which are secrets. Secrecy, as far as we know, is a purely human trait; it is difficult to imagine other animals having secret, creative tendencies with unstated agendas. The notion of 'secrecy' used here is defined by an architect's deliberate exclusion (or

2 Although architects may believe in society's need for more ritual, they will not necessarily convey this view to a client if they feel the client will not be receptive to the idea. It may be acted on during the evolution of the client's project, but it may not be made explicit. The architect may, however, describe this aspect of the building (one of its secrets) to architectural students in a lecture, and some of them may start to see the world as a manifestation of ritualistic activities about which they had previously been ignorant.

concealment) of his or her full objectives from the client. But sometimes a drawing or text can hold accidental secrets that are obscure even to their creator.

What is it about architecture that compels an architect to become a double or triple agent, a conspirator conspiring with more than one conspiracy? Why is it that honesty is not the best policy? Does honesty exist culturally? Are these secrets to do with embarrassment, one-upmanship, or something deeper in our nature? These are some of the questions that need to be answered so that the profession can see itself in the light of cultural ambiguity.

Paradoxical Practice

Successful architects are immediately caught in a paradox. Architecture is itself a mixture of bifurcating aspirations, by necessity both poetic and pragmatic. Architects keep secrets from each other in order to get on; they set out their narrative stalls and exclude many of their beliefs and aspirations in order to make these stalls attractive to the 'other'. As a tactic in the achievement of personal objectives, this behaviour encourages common interaction or conversation (a type of reconnaissance), although it is always heavy with nuances perceived or postulated by an active mind. Secrecy allows architects to experiment; after all, they practise by entertaining globally unacceptable concepts for exploration. They all project spatial and material configurations that are new to them (P-creativity). A second architectural paradox (one of many) is the clash between professional and theoretical experimental ideals.[3] Professionalism insists that 'practising' architects are scientifically and empirically in con-

3 In her book *The Creative Mind* (Cardinal, 1990), Margaret Boden writes of the existence of two types of creativity: H-creativity and P-creativity. P-creativity is a personal creative discovery, new to us but not to others. H-creativity is an historical creative discovery, new to the sum of human knowledge – relativity, for example.

digital dreams

trol at all steps of the work, whereas theoretical experimentation insists that they are not. 'The secret' allows aspirations and emotions about buildings and site that are instigated, perhaps, but not bought by a client's payments or political status. In a world where the majority of building is concerned with delivering a purely functional product on time and within budget, the secret seems to be an advantage. When an architect is caught in a web of commercial sophism, the notion of the drawing as a secret laboratory, visible yet partly invisible, can be helpful.

Imitating Other Selfish Nests

The laboratory of the drawing is akin to the scientist's Petri dish, a place where memes can be grown and tested. If the architectural drawing is seen as the product of a Joycean meme-nest – in effect, a virtual machine for running memetic software[4] – one could conclude that its *modus operandi* will fluctuate according to which memetic software is running. The drawing has, therefore, the ability to bury secrets, with access limited to the holder of the relevant memetic software. This software could, however, be hacked. One of the main teaching vehicles in architectural education is the 'crit', which in some sense is ordered to allow critics to unpick, question or debate a portion of a student's graphic tracings, part of his or her meme-nest. Once a student understands some of the opportunities that can be posited by this system of reading and rereading – for example,

4 The notion of the virtual machine of the mind and memetic software is part of Daniel Dennett's thesis on consciousness. On page 210 of his *Consciousness Explained* (Penguin, 1991), this theory is succinctly expressed: 'Human consciousness is itself a huge complex of memes (or, more exactly, meme effects in brains) that can best be understood as the operation of a "von Neumannesque" virtual machine implemented in the parallel architecture of a brain that was not designed for any such activities. The powers of this virtual machine vastly enhance the underlying powers of the organic hardware on which it runs, but at the same time many of its most curious features, especially its limitations, can be explained as the byproducts of the kludges that make possible this curious but effective reuse of an existing organ for novel purposes.'

meaning in architecture is

by learning to understand a shuffled meme-pack thrown on to the surface of a drawing – creativity takes on a more considered and powerful direction. To trace the memic dogfight and to chart individual memes and their possible influence on a proposal is indeed an architectural skill.

Drawing is a risk. The intricacies of a drawing are therapeutic and can reveal ways out of even a complex meme cluster. Drawing allows the architect to experience the fear and ecstasy of the painter. To confront a blank canvas or paper is an act of violence, a defying of whiteness and of absence; the exposure of the meme (the first mark) in the necessary no man's land of the drawing is feared by surface and artist alike. In making this mark, the artist is committed to completion, and to a spiritual nagging until it has been achieved. The architect must know these fears and treat them with respect, for they will reveal opportunities previously inconceivable. When we consider the theory of consciousness proposed by Daniel Dennett in his book *Consciousness Explained*,5 we see that there is an analogy between Dennett's virtual machine of the mind and the virtual machine of the drawing. Further, we can see that we run virtual software on both, searching for answers to our problems and to satisfy our conceptions of reality. Nothing is certain or concrete because we are always mentally preparing the next draft.6 Because the hardware of the drawing – the ink, the collage, the film, the tracing paper – has not evolved fast enough to complement the variety of concepts now open to us, we must constantly work in allegory.

The drawing is a way of primitively recording the body's creative trance; it is akin to a ritualistic

5 See note 4.

6 On page 111 of *Consciousness Explained*, Dennett discusses the Multiple Drafts model of consciousness: 'I expect it will seem quite alien and hard to visualise at first – that's how entrenched the Cartesian Theater idea is. According to the Multiple Drafts model, all varieties of perception – indeed, all varieties of thought and mental activity – are accomplished in the brain by parallel, multitrack processes of interpretation and elaboration of sensory inputs. Information entering the nervous system is under continuous "editorial revision".'

digital dreams

glasgow

tower

and

the

impermanence

of

meaning

constantly shifting

No conscious effort has been made to be contextual, for context will become less and less defined during the new millennium. Technology defies context, it is ubiquitous; perception will be less and less linked to place.

The tower is planned within a surreal park which includes elevated hedges, a chrome crescent-shaped sky, the contortions of the bus station and four enigmatic sculptures. These sculptures contain virtually real images of other cities: millennium towers that are 'scratch-mixed' into images of the real tower and the surreal park, gleaned from the constantly moving cameras that traverse the site on steel wires. The resultant mix of images and sensations negates contextual criteria.

The tower itself (lift, showroom and hotel) is hung with ephemera and sited on the corrupted axis; it affords spectacular views of Glasgow from its huge restaurant/viewing gallery/ dance floor/conference facility. The elevated hedges plunge through the foyer space, punctuating it with high-level landscape and giving a taste of the other landscape interventions further up the building.

The tower is dressed: it will forever change its clothes as the impermanence of meaning constantly changes all we see.

shaman's dance that unveils a journey into the realm of the gods. The architectural secret is a secret even to its creator at this early stage. The result is a drawn text containing allegorical marks defining the complex physical and emotional context in which it is drawn. Contrary to popular belief, architecture on paper is not safe; it is a place where secrets are either told or kept. Such drawings are a personal cartography, a map of intentions on a quest for creative identity. The conditions of society, site and drawing meet as the architect becomes a social and personal condenser, with the drawing a mixing-desk for secret music. Some mapped memes have 'frequency-dependent fitness' and their strength is conditioned by a dependency on being held in a minority of meme-nests (masonic societies and the architectural avant-garde are two such examples). Some macro-memes create nested-meme space: the meme for 'architect' creates a fertile breeding ground for 'architectural drawing' and consequently the 'perspective' meme, and so on.

The Architectural Prisoner's Dilemma

The level of the drawing surface is where the secret's integrity is compromised. The compromise which is the drawing is a result of the inability of nested memes to ascertain effectively their weaknesses and their dependency on other meme types. Implicit in the act of drawing is a psychological cleansing during which secrets are confessed. The meme for 'personal architectural lexicon' combined with the meme for 'architectural egotism' often creates arrogance in architects. Weighed down with secrets, they court isolation and are self-goaded into exploring fully a personal memetic space in their search for the unique (H-creativity) – a search for a few hybrid or mutant

meaning in architecture is

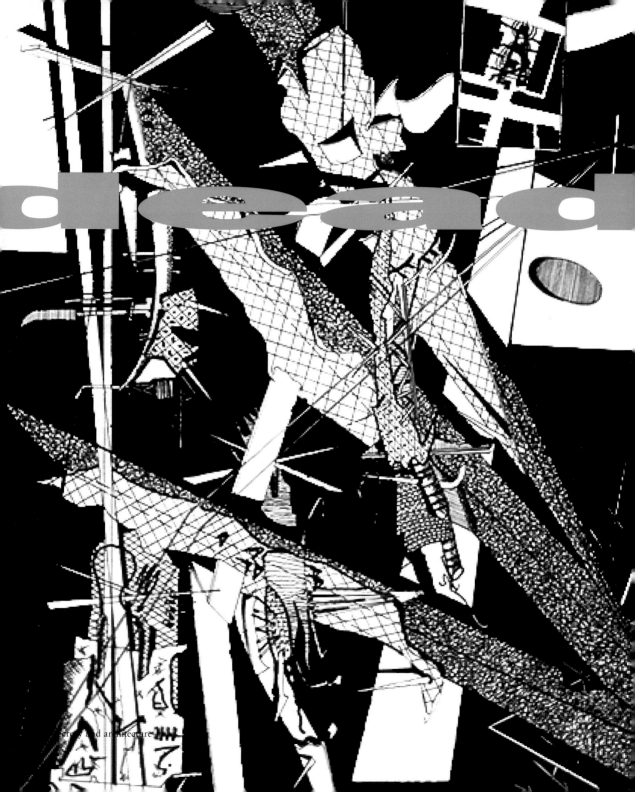

dead

secrecy and architecture

memes from which uniqueness might stem. Within the creative loneliness of architects no re-enactment of proven solutions will suffice, nor can they rest on the laurels of uninspired success. A secret idea is one that wells up from the subconscious, conditioned by the memetic space of the individual. The innate wickedness of plagiarism would consign the perpetrator to the crowded back-benches of the profession. To avoid this plague the architect is forced to become a creative escapologist, with the drawing a concealed key. The drawing is a mystic sea ready to be charted, providing reference points to the secrecy and sanctuary of the mind. As the Joycean creative mind rambles on forever, making draft after draft, with practicality limping mockingly behind, the architect must be able to transform a beautiful idea into reality, plucking it out of the air like a conjuror on an empty stage. A scheme that is not realised has a sadness to it; it is stillborn, a multidimensional idea imprisoned in two dimensions,7 its memes unable to replicate to the best of their ability. To achieve buildings that are cool lullabies or stormbringers, architects must be able to make multidimensional decisions. To create buildings in time and space that are sublime, they must battle the forces of normality and naïve realism and convey their secret to its rightful end.

7 The drawing is not the only casket that imprisons an idea by confining its dimensions; in architecture, any traditional representational device limits an idea by its lack of dimensionality.

For architects, the drawing is at first the only act of creation in the visible world, their way of impregnation, of furthering their cause – a means to an end or the end of a meme. Secrecy is the architect's only friend.

Architects want to infest your mind! For what other reason would they draw and write? No more can be revealed; it is a secret!

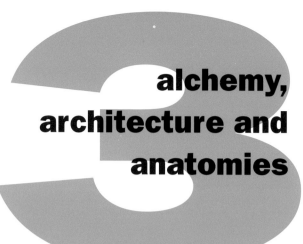

alchemy, architecture and anatomies

When magic becomes
scientific fact we refer to
it as medicine or
astronomy.
    Anton La Vey

Only an architectural Luddite would disagree that architecture is the subject of constant transmutation. This transmutation is necessary for achitecture's continued centrality in respect to society. The frequency and amplitude of these changes are becoming extreme.

This chapter charts the similarities between architecture and alchemy, and examines two of the major issues of culture, and hence architecture: the fluctuating status of the image and the changing nature of the body – as perceived through an alchemic lens (architecture after the 'orgy', as Baudrillard would have us believe[1]).

Brushing Aside the Coat of Skins

One of the ways to observe the constant transmutation of architecture is to strip aside the 'coat of skins' that it has accumulated and reveal its mythologies – and thus its true nature – in an attempt to find the elusive 'stuff' of architecture.

Where does one start on such a quest? The road to architectural nirvana is a long one, fraught with false starts, misconceptions, ugliness and stupidity. Architecture has always been synonymous with myth, ritual, history and tradition,[2] yet at the end of the twentieth century it finds itself concerned with mobility and perception; digital, smart, soft and wet technologies and information; and cross-cultural inspiration. How can these supposed opposites be reconciled? How can these factors be combined and transformed into vital architectures for the twenty-first century?

1 J Baudrillard, *The Transparency of Evil, Essays on Extreme Phenomena*, trans. J Benedict, Verso, 1993. Baudrillard sees the 'orgy' of modernism as an explosion of liberation; his thesis is that any progress of thought in any type of human endeavour is condemned to the tyranny of the simulation. 'The goals of liberation are already behind us.'

2 Ritual, perhaps, seems an anachronistic concept; however, ritual continues to cast its many spells over our world – the State opening of Parliament, buying a round of drinks, Christmas, the key to the door at eighteen, are just a few current examples. Ritual has affected the art of architecture throughout the ages. Conditioned by so much ritual in our society, architecture must contain a spiritual nature. In history we learn about

the representational tactics that have been adopted by architects and master builders to integrate symbolic elements of ritual into their structures. We look at Stonehenge and see a map of the druid's esoteric practices and his perceived relationship with the cosmos. In a similar way we can interpret Aztec temples, cathedrals, the pyramids and so on – up to the present day. Further, architecture is not just a vehicle for the encapsulation of myth; architecture itself has mythic qualities. At this point it is, perhaps, useful to define 'myth'. A myth is a story embodying and declaring a pattern of relationships between humanity, other forms of life and the environment. One man's myth is another's religion. Architecture is polytheistic; that is, it does not adhere to one god but many. The gods are paradigms.

Our quest for a valid starting point that might give hints of this 'other' architecture must be analogous with architecture itself. We must search in the present for a clue from the past and a sign for the future, a memory of something forgotten yet useful, something to read with the lens of modernity, a way to do and a way to find.

It is here that we find alchemy, the art of transformation – both spiritual and physical, micro- and macrocosmic. Alchemy is cryptic, esoteric, a reconciler of opposites, engaged in by mavericks and charlatans, discredited and supposedly superfluous – much like our beloved art of architecture.

The Black Art

Alchemy is not merely similar to architecture; with our current and future technologies the two are one and the same. The alchemic analogy is useful in pointing the way to possible spatial chemistries that just might free us from architectural deadlock. Our technologies are alchemic in their ability to reconfigure matter; the more science progresses, the more alchemically adept we become.

Throughout its history, alchemy has been regarded as either the highest of studies or the domain of fraudsters and fools. Its evolution has been influenced by Chinese mysticism in the East and Graeco-Arabic civilisation in the West. After the Dark Ages, the Europeans began to develop alchemy, combining its mysticism with Christian theology. The Renaissance then triggered a renewed pursuit of the subject and alchemy became the mainstay of many esoteric philosophies. The study of alchemy has always been draped in mystery, allegory and symbolism (the word 'gibberish', used to describe the cryptic writings of the adept Geber, is in fact alchemic in origin).

digital dreams

Drawings are held in position by dissecting needles and pointed rivets, a recognition of the fluid process of architectural design caught and pinned in a moment of static splendour, where abstraction meets representation.

The work consists of seven drawings in six parts, each separate but dependent on the whole: integrity yet cohesion. The drawings are entitled:

1 The Slough of Despond

2 Bain-Marie (She's Got a Whalebone Smile)

3 The Dragon Tower

4 The Royal Alembic

5 The Rebis (The Falling Ewel)

6 The Alkahest

7 The Secret

Although adepts were keen to preserve the secret of the true nature of their art, many of alchemy's concepts were assimilated into the practice of other disciplines such as medicine, music and literature, as well as chemistry.

Alchemy almost disappeared nearly three centuries ago, but there has always been an interest in its literature and art. Nearer the present day, the surrealists were inspired by alchemic and other occult literature to produce some of their most memorable works – Duchamp's *The Bride Stripped Bare by her Bachelors, Even* (*The Large Glass*), and Ernst's *Of This Man Shall Know Nothing* and *The Robing of the Bride*, for example. It is interesting to reflect here on the principles of alchemic thought that so excited the surrealists:

1 The universe is a single, live entity.

2 The universe comprises powerful opposites.

3 The microcosm of these opposites is the sexes.

4 Imagination is the true motivating force of the universe, and can act on matter.

5 Mind and matter are the same.

6 Self-realisation that yields an understanding of the cosmos comes through intuitive thought, chance, self-induced derangement or experimentation.[3]

An alchemist has been described as someone who brings about a succession of changes in the material he works with, transforming it from a gross, unrefined state into a perfect and purified form. His 'gold' is not only real metal but the Philosopher's Stone, the Lapis (enlightenment). The metallurgical analogy is both the means of encryption into which

3 N Choucha, *Surrealism and the Occult*, Mandrake, 1991. Choucha sees much of the work of the key personalities within the dada and surrealist movements (Kandinsky, Dali, Ernst, Picasso and Duchamp, for example) as manifestations of an interest in the occult, particularly alchemy and shamanism. This interest was commonly paralleled by a preoccupation with psychology.

alchemy, architecture and anatomies

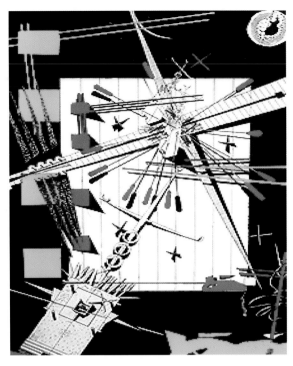

The Slough of Despond

At times of creative block, the Slough of Despond (perhaps known by the architect as well as anyone) is the place where solutions are secret and invisible, the void where the creative self confronts new pressures. The two old opposites – the biological and the mechanical – are again unresolved, with the microcosm their site. The kiln of the drawing is used as a reliquary for the redundant and the mistaken, but through the heat of drawing comes an understanding of the complexity of the opposites and the levels of their priority and fusion.

the secrets of The Great Work are encoded and the anthropocentric operation of its ritual: the scale of the microcosm. The gold is also understood as man's search for perfection of spirit. Alchemy has been practised by many influential people, including Francis Bacon, Isaac Newton and Robert Boyle, and without it their achievements may not have reached such celebrated heights.

The initial step in the alchemic work is to discover the prima materia, the Slough of Despond, the scum and filth of the world. Many clues to its identity are to be found in alchemic texts, but the secret has never been known outside the world of the adepts, who, indeed, experimented with numerous substances deemed to be the elusive material. It was said that the prima materia was overlooked by man, almost invisible to him, and this inspired many a medieval alchemist to investigate an assortment of base substances – immortalised by Chaucer in *The Canon Yeoman's Tale* as 'poudres diverse, asshes, dong, pisse and cley'. Other substances thought to contain the prima materia were blood, hair, bones, spittle, semen, soil, worms and dew. In a typical eulogy to the prima materia, it is 'familiar to all men, both young and old, is found in the country, in the village, in the town, in all things created by God; yet it is despised by all. Rich and poor handle it every day … no one prizes it, though, next to the human soul, it is the most precious thing upon the earth and has the power to pull down kings and princes. Nevertheless it is esteemed the vilest and meanest of earthly things.'[4]

4 C Gilchrist, *Elements of Alchemy*, Element Books, 1991, p. 41: an excellent beginner's guide to alchemic concepts, an introduction to the rich mythic world of alchemy and alchemic graphic representation.

digital dreams

Contemporary developments in the scientific understanding of matter suggest that, essentially, all matter is space at various interacting curvatures. Here, at the outset of the alchemic opus, it can be seen that alchemy and architecture share a fundamental basis – the manipulation of space in all its varied forms, philosophical and physical. Once the prima materia is established, a process of considerable complexity is undertaken and must be strictly adhered to. Crucial aspects include the timing of events, zodiacal orientation, the equipment used, and the spiritual attitude of the alchemist. The prima materia is manipulated chemically, usually by means of heat and distillation, until it eventually reaches a complete state. This process can take years, during which time distillation of a liquid can occur many hundreds of times.

The outward appearance of the prima materia must be destroyed by fire or acidic solutions. The composite opposites, sometimes called the King and Queen or the Dragons, are set against one another. In architecture the resolution of disparate parameters – such as site, ecology, programme, accommodation and the urban grain – is the first step in the process of dealing with space (the prima materia). In alchemy these opposites are reconciled by the chemical wedding, or the marriage between King and Queen. Further work on the substance provokes the 'death' of the material, also called the nigredo. But the soul of the matter is still contained in the alembic (the glass vessel which holds the material during the process) and must be made visible. This series of events is called the conjunctio, the incestuous (because they are brother and sister) union of the King and Queen. Once coupling has occurred, death swiftly follows and the mixture enters a state of putrefaction. From this decomposition is born

Bain-Marie (she's got a whalebone smile)

The Bain-Marie is the warm bath of alchemy, the site of washing and baptism and the purification of the creative urge: a point of new beginning. The formal nature of the drawing conjures images of both the Earth Mother and a gothic, mandalic vault. It also suggests the mystic sister or brother, or the personality of the shadow (as Jung would have it). Our shadow-self is the aspect of our personality that we all seek to conceal.[1] The Bain-Marie is a portal both in architecture and in alchemy: the wet door to revelation.

1 R A Johnson, in *Owning Your Own Shadow, Understanding the Dark Side of the Psyche* (HarperCollins, 1991), explains simply the concept of the shadow-self. 'The Shadow: what is this curious dark element that follows us like a saurian tail and pursues us so relentlessly in our psychological world? What role does it occupy in the modern psyche?'

the androgyny, the child of the King and Queen. This resurrection is also called the 'Peacock's Tail', an eruption of bright colour from which white emerges (white light is the integrated mix of all the colours of the spectrum). The white stone is the first stage of the elixir; after further manipulation the whiteness reddens to produce the red rose or the gold, the culmination of the process.

The alchemic opus contains many lessons and perspectives on aspects of architecture that may prove useful to those whose thinking is aimed at the future. As science approaches eastern mysticism,[5] science and nature will at last become reconciled.

5 F Capra, *The Tao of Physics*, Flamingo, 1983: Capra's seminal work on the evolving concepts in quantum physics and the parallels to be found in many eastern religions.

Image Addiction

The alchemic process is one of transformation brought about by the synthesis of material and concepts, and the distillation of their essence. Since the halcyon days of alchemy, the existential collage of life and information has become more and more complex. The feudal serf's 'reality' consisted of the seasons, local geography, basic feudal politics, religion, sex and gossip. Compared to this, our existence is more of a hyperreality. Every day our knowledge is informed by the global communication nets, travel, and the constant dance of millions of images. The dadaist collage of our contemporary existence is made up of increasingly smaller and smaller components – sound bites and image 'blips'. While the prima materia of architecture and alchemy is space, space cannot exist without information. In architecture one needs to conceive of the container of space to perceive the space. As in alchemy, the negative must be seen in order to view the positive. Two objects set close together must reveal

digital dreams

The Dragon Tower and the Royal Alembic

Opposites to be reconciled are sometimes called warring dragons. The Dragon Tower (crucifix in plan, section and elevation) is weighed down with iron tears – a site of murder and resurrection. It is here that opposites are resolved: the King and Queen are combined in sexual coupling, the marital bed bathed in water. The architectural idea, attractive yet only half-born in the alembic of the mind, is a spark of optimism before the despondency of rejection and the nothingness of the nigredo.

The Alkahest

The rebis travels into the second alembic, deep into the darkness below ground. It is here that the belly hungrily awaits sustenance, its digestive fluids the 'grey goo' of nanotechnology.[2] The alchemic alkahest is the liquid panacea, the elixir of life. If ever a contemporary alkahest has been postulated, it is the molecular-scaled assemblers and replicators of this theory. The rebis plunges into the nanovat to be turned molecule by molecule into gold. The alchemist watches from the cosseting egg, dumbstruck by the beauty of the gold and the realisation that the time of alchemy has arrived, together with its mystic sister, architecture. The gold then returns to its rebis form and is dragged from the alkahest. The whole process is then reversed and the cyclic nature of the alchemic tradition is made manifest in the machinery of building.

The architects of the future will have nano engineering at their disposal. This will enable them to produce an architecture of flux, of cyclic distillations effected by the personal attitudes of users, the natural cycles and differing scales of action. The mechanical and the organic will be reconciled by the transformation of the prima materia of architecture and alchemy: space. Subtle manipulations of space at an atomic level will produce astounding changes at higher scales. This will influence human perception itself.

2 G Bear, *Blood Music*, Legend, 1988.

digital dreams

The Rebis (The Falling Ewel)

The Rebis first makes itself felt by the destructive act of plummeting from on high and shattering the marital bed, flinging to the winds all that has so far been achieved. The falling ewel is the Black Death, the end but a new beginning. It is both murderer and redeemer. It knows many names. It is a double thing yet its form is indeterminate. Its impact initiates the nigredo, but terminates it once it splashes into the alkahest.

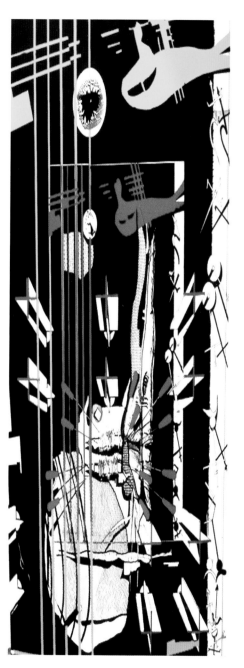

information about their form and content if we are to understand the space in between them. In the 'cyberblitz' of information, reconciliation of concepts in the hermetic vessel of the mind becomes crucial, for the cognitive map of life is both personal and varied.

We have become a 'blip' society, addicted to image and spectacle. The concept of a cyclic distillation is becoming more and more powerful in our time, as images are digitally morphed, sampled and synthesised and ejected into the feedback loop of global society, a society which is excreting and consuming information at a frightening rate. The architect's work will be deconstructed, reconstructed and offered up for fresh consumption. The image has become a virus. Once it has been produced virally, the image infects, invading and asserting its own agenda; it is then further reproduced and projected on to the screen of the mind, any mind – or its macrocosm, the city.

Trashing the Flesh Cage

Technologies are becoming better life-support systems for our images than for our bodies. IMAGES ARE IMMORTAL. BODIES ARE EPHEMERAL. The body finds it increasingly difficult to match the expectations of its images. In the realm of multiplying and morphing images, the physical body's impotence is apparent.

THE BODY PERFORMS BEST AS ITS IMAGE.

Stelarc (performance artist)

Strangely – or not so strangely, depending on your view of scientific hubris – technology has consistently eroded the established relationship between mind and body. At various points in history, this relationship has been abruptly re-articulated.

alchemy, architecture and anatomies

6 C G Jung, in *Psychology and Alchemy* (Routledge, 1953, p. 4), states that 'There is in the analytical process, that is to say in the dialectical discussion between the conscious mind and the unconscious, a development or an advance towards some goal or end.' Jung analysed the alchemic tradition in terms of a semiotic parallel to the current issues in the psychology of the self.

The containment parameters of body and mind,[6] and their expansion by successive orders of technology, have crucially altered the state of humanity.

Alchemy teaches us that great changes can be wrought by small manipulations of substance. To chart these manipulations and fluctuations we must consider the history and future of the technological prosthetic. Architecture is a man-made carapace of the body; changes in or of body therefore necessitate a sympathetic, altered architecture. The increasing effectiveness with which we are able to dissolve the body into new technological realms calls for a completely different architecture. Such architecture will be not only in the natural container of the 'real' world, but also in the quantum and digital arenas. The issue of the site of the prosthesis seems inextricably linked to the change in the state of both body and architecture. The prosthesis is an agent for the alchemy of transmutation, the solvent of architecture.

The evolution of the prosthetic began in prehistoric times, when man started to use tools.[7] The first mechanical prosthetic came about when an object was imbued with a different functionality. This was swiftly followed by the honing of the object to augment its new-found effectiveness. These simple prosthetics, such as a rock used as a hammer, expanded man's

7 B Mazlish, *The Fourth Discontinuity, the Co-evolution of Man and Machines*, Yale, 1993, p. 220: 'Out of humanity comes machines.' Freud's view was that machines have turned men into 'prosthetic Gods'.

sphere of influence. At this level, the site of the mechanical prosthetic is one of adjacency to the body. The prosthetic fluctuates from site to site, and with each higher technologic distillation it moves to higher orders of site by adjacency and reduction of scale, even to the point of invisibility. Currently, the site of the prosthetic exists simultaneously on many levels

digital dreams

and at many locations; it is both a ubiquity and a particularity.[8] Today, the mechanical prosthetic, highly evolved from the rude stone-as-hammer concept, exists as a device external to the body in the form of glasses, false limbs and hearing aids. With contact lenses the prosthetic penetrates the surface; and with heart pacemakers and alloy hip-joints, it is actually inside the body.

Evolving in parallel with the mechanical prosthetic was its biological counterpart, triggered off by the advent of animal and plant husbandry. The site of the biological prosthetic has also fluctuated – from outside the body to its surface (with the utilisation of skins for clothing), and then to within the body itself (with the harvesting of blood, plasma, organs and antitoxins for the purpose of placement in another body). One type of prosthetic can be dependent on another for its acceptance, as in the case of a transplanted organ and an anti-rejection drug.

This introduces the pharmaceutical prosthetic, which also has a long history, from witchdoctors' potions, through the discovery of alcohol, to the complex pharmaceuticals we use today. The complexity of the body's cellular components necessitates a reduction in scale of the prosthetic, and it is for this reason that the nanoscopic becomes important. With complex long-chain molecules bumping around the maelstrom of the body in search of a sister molecule to bond with or to destroy, consciousness now becomes an issue. No one will deny that drinking alcohol changes perception. Chemical prosthetics can offer an altered perception of personal space. As the history of the shaman illustrates, there have always been attempts to control and navigate narcotic space.

8 D Zohar, *The Quantum Self*, Bloomsbury, 1990. Zohar uses the analogy of the quantum hussy to explain the ubiquity of the electron cloud and, indeed, each electron within it.

The Royal Alembic

The Royal Alembic (the glass vessel) holds the marital bed/coffin at its centre, surrounded by the bird fountains of recurring distillation. It is simultaneously functional and symbolic, both sun and moon, with the alchemic crucifix operating on a variety of levels at the same time.

The Secret

In alchemy there is always something not told. This drawing contains all future architectural schemes, but sadly they are invisible to us. All possibilities are shrouded in a veil of whiteness. Our search for the sublime is seen through clouded vision.

A further shift in the site of the prosthetic occurred with the invention – or should I say 'discovery' – of access to cyberspace. This has created the digital prosthetic, whose site has now moved to the non-place of computer software, rendering the prosthetic invisible or 'virtual'. It might now be possible for the self to discard the oldest prosthetic of all, the body. With the cyberspace prosthetic it may be possible to escape the 'meat' for good, with no harm caused. This 'crossover'9 is aided by the possibility that the mind could be understood as purely digital – and could therefore be separated from its host body. It is at this point – when the prosthetic has been mastered and man is able to achieve the mental transmutability predicted in alchemy – that cries of incredulity and outrage will be heard concerning the sacrosanct nature of human consciousness.10 And, indeed, this area of scientific research does throw up issues more complex than the use of a hammer.

9 P Cadigan, 'Pretty Boy Crossover', in *Best Science Fiction*, Fourth Annual Collection, ed. G Dozois, St Martins, New York, 1987. A science-fiction story concerning the transition from real to unreal space and the downloading of human consciousness.

10 The consciousness debate is currently at the leading edge of psychology and artificial intelligence. The battle lines are drawn: one side maintains that human consciousness can or will be explained and quantified; the other argues that it cannot and will not. An article that sets out clearly the parameters of this argument is 'The Consciousness Wars' by Robert K J Killheffer in *Omni*, Science and the Soul, Fifteenth Anniversary Collectors' Edition, October 1993.

The cyberspace prosthetic also hails the end of site-specificity for architecture. With this particular distillation of technology, the prosthetic and the alchemic analogy reach an intensity previously unattainable.

Cyberspace is revelatory by nature; it is magic, a master of

digital dreams

appearance and disappearance. Cyberspace creates a techno-animism:[11] God is in the matrix and omnipresent. In the future, objects stumbled upon in cyberspace may be conscious. A resurrection of architecture is required that is liberated from time, services and tectonic structure. The prosthetic can be seen as the means to achieve a compaction of time and space, resulting in less time spent on tasks that are both adjacent and remote (in cyberspace, objects can occupy the same space at the same time). However, one man's cyberspatial realm could be another's madness.

At our current rate of technological acceleration, the difference between near future and deep future may be just fifty years. Once the downloading of human personality has been achieved, the possibility of software resurrection in cyberspace could be augmented by a mechanical resurrection in 'real' space.

Hans Moravec has postulated the manufacture of 'bush' robots, fractally branching mechanisms capable of experiencing the world on a micro- and macroscopic scale simultaneously. The cyberspace prosthetic has allowed us to visualise, manipulate and splice molecules. Where this occurs in DNA the consequent genetic engineering creates the genetic prosthetic, a further process in man's accelerating ability to transmutate. Here the genetic prima materia of the DNA code is bathed in segments of imported code in the hope that the alien piece will become integrated into the genetic chain. Such genetic engineering has resulted in pigs, cattle and mice with human genes. And once again, the site of the prosthetic is shifted. The prosthetic becomes ubiquitous, sited within the

11 Animism is the notion that God dwells within, or is in an object or an animal. This belief, identified by the anthropologist E B Tylor, is found in many religions. An example of animism is that God is (in) the mountain. Strangely, for architects, 'God is in the details' (if we adhere to the often repeated adage of Mies van der Rohe).

Image Addiction

In a search for 'blippyness', the drawing is morphed, spliced, fragmented and collaged. The unforeseen becomes seeable. A dadaist synaesthesia reveals the simultaneous and gratuitous coexistence of an infinite number of perceptual frames. This new fluidity consists of the thick line of suggestion and the thin line of the specific. A thousand outcomes are possible in every brushstroke. The prima materia is discovered, ready for distillation; its virus is embedded in your stream of consciousness, in a different form from its sister in mine. The fabric of your screen is not the same as the fabric of mine.

body of both the donor and the recipient of the gene. Transgeneticism, as this is called, will obviously generate copious ethical debate. Many people find the quantifiability of genetic engineering repugnant. However, the history of the prosthetic is bound with use and abuse, and any invention or discovery inevitably brings with it new accidents and potential abuses.[12] These must all be debated and, if necessary, legislated against.

The current 'slap-dash' method for the placement of alien genes is becoming more predictable as our knowledge of the Human Genome is quantified. It is interesting to note that the alchemic opus has been reflected in the process of mitosis (cell multiplication) and hence in the gestation of all living things.[13]

A prosthetic of the future is the nanoprosthetic. It is born out of the theoretical notion of nanotechnology and is, perhaps, the penultimate prosthetic. It may well represent the final transmutation of the human frame, mental and physical. Nanotechnology treats molecules and atoms as very small factories, where each atom is part of a programme unit or robotic arm or replicator.[14] Here at last the biological and the mechanical are reconciled. Literally anything is possible with nanotechnology because it acts out programmed displacements of atoms one by one, with small changes bringing about huge changes of state on a larger scale. Obviously, again, the potential for abuse, or even loss of control, is frightening. The loss-of-control

12 In the book *Pure War*, Paul Virilio states that 'every technology produces, provokes and programs a specific accident'.

13 J Fabricius, *Alchemy*, Aquarian Press, 1989. Fabricius takes readers through the gestation period of the foetus and likens it to the stages of the alchemic process.

14 The theoretical background to nanotechnology, its huge potential and some of its effects on life, are explained in K Eric Drexler's *Engines of Creation*, Oxford University Press, 1990.
Two of the renowned pioneers of artificial intelligence are Alan Turing and John von Neumann. Turing is best known for his test for ascertaining artificial intelligence (subsequently called the Turing Test) and his mathematical proof of the Universal Computer (the Turing Machine). Von Neumann's contribution to the field was his work regarding automata theory and machine self-reproduction.

digital dreams

Trashing the Flesh Cage

Here the body of the drawing is seen through an 'other' lens, a type of x-ray which sees beyond and into the flesh of the work. This lens reveals the mechanical and the biological continually in flux as the site of the prosthetic changes. The components of the drawing, never predictable, change as the flesh becomes victim to the dance of the prosthetic – the angular and the fluid parodying the biological and the mechanical. The body of the drawing is transformed by the continual shifting relationship between host and parasite as they evolve through a process of symbiosis into a hybrid organism, its opposites reconciled in a never-ending progression to omega.

scenario is graphically illustrated by Greg Bear in his science-fiction novel *Blood Music*,[15] which documents the evolution of biotechnical organisms that escape human control.[16] The effect of a nanotechnological revolution will be devastating and will change the nature of humanity beyond all recognition. Scientists call this point in time, when the nano revolution has taken its toll, the omega point. Some scientists believe that at the omega point man will have complete knowledge of the universe,[17] synonymous, perhaps, with the finding of the Philosopher's Stone, the alchemist's 'gold'. This would bring the frightening powers of God within our grasp.

Even if architecture regains its centrality to human endeavour and continues to run hand-in-hand with biological (or even nano) man to the end of atomic time, there will still be yet one more prosthetic to invent – the final, post-atomic prosthetic. Provisionally, the human race is doomed to extinction at the time of the heat death of the universe. This is predicted to be 1031 years (the life-span of photons of light) into the future. To vault this gaping chasm, man will need to become post-atomic. It has been postulated that we may be

15 G Bear, *Blood Music*, op. cit. This science-fiction scenario of biotechnology running wild illustrates effectively the worries of viral infection, the 'grey goo' problem, and conscious biomechanical machines.

16 Self-replicating nanotechnological machines have an exponential reproduction curve; if these machines were left unchecked, the world could be overrun by 'grey goo' in a matter of hours. Consequently, the issue of software control is crucial, both the writing of it at this scale and our ability to ensure its integrity and security.

17 E Regis, *Great Mambo Chicken and the Transhuman Condition*, Viking, 1991. Regis charts a course through some of the most hubristic scientific thoughts in recent years and introduces readers to the unnerving lengths scientists will go to in order to validate their ideas. Cryonics, downloading and post-biological man are among the concepts explored.

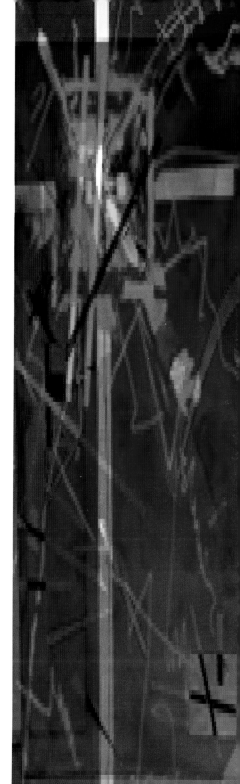

able to survive by inhabiting electronic plasma. But what will be the architecture of electronic plasma?[18] Perhaps this, truly, will be the alchemic moment of revelation. Only one thing is sure: at any stage in our evolution we cannot escape the concept of transmutation. And the creation and viability of architecture are inextricably tied to it.

[18] Regis, ibid.

digital dreams

tripping the light fantastic

He turned one of his power rings, disseminating the sky, the lightning, the thunder, replacing them with pearly clouds, radiated with golden light through which silvery rain still fell.

'And now,' he murmured, 'I give you Tranquillity, and in Tranquillity – Hope ...'

A further twist of the ring and a rainbow appeared, bridging the chasm, touching the clouds. Bishop Castle was impressed by what was an example of elegance rather than spectacle ...

Michael Moorcock, *Legends from the End of Time*

Have you ever believed in something that has turned out to be a lie? We are now in the midst of the greatest lie that has been told by man to man. It concerns the stealing of our inviolate sense of reality, the mixing of substance with absence, and the fracturing of our sense of being; but, as with all good lies, we like it. Our history is full of stories and myths whose narratives are dependent on mystical, magical environments. These surreal environments and dreams are now becoming crystal clear and interactive. They are easily communicated and duplicated. This lie is the conspiracy of cyberspace (ironically, a word coined on an old mechanistic typewriter before it disappeared into a museum, which will itself at some point disappear). Let's get one thing straight: cyberspace is an overused word. It seems to have been applied to anything that contains a printed circuit. Pundits have defined various cyberspaces, one example being 'the space where you are when you are on the phone'. In this book, cyberspace refers to the spatial qualities produced by being able to virtually (bodily) inhabit computer memories and/or environments.

The architectural profession is going to have to face up to the incredible stress that this new access will inflict on the nature of architecture and architects. This potential is groundbreaking in more senses than one. Let us take a few sips from this heady concoction of cybernet Sauvignon.

In the beginning there was the Word and the Word was cyberspace. The word first appeared in the 'Genesis' of the cyberspatial bible, *Neuromancer,* and provided the backdrop to a trilogy of novels by the science-fiction author William Gibson.[1] These novels have done more than anything else to contribute to the evolving mythology of the non-placed Utopia

1 W Gibson, *Neuromancer*, Victor Gollancz Ltd, 1984; *Count Zero*, Victor Gollancz Ltd, 1986; *Mona Lisa Overdrive*, Grafton, 1989.

the holon house Architects are ideally placed to conceive of methods of ordering

of cyberspace. Cyberspace is the place that is no place, the space of computer simulation, currently accessed by virtual-reality headgear, the modem, the data glove, and the lap- and palm-top.

Imagine a world where all is possible, where time and space are fragmented and reconfigured in non-linear formats. Before the advent of most of the computerised hardware and software prosthetics that populate our environment today, Michael Moorcock wrote *Legends from the End of Time*,[2] a novel which describes a world, just before Apoca-

2 M Moorcock, *Legends from the End of Time*, W H Allen & Co. Ltd, 1976.

lypse, where the few remaining survivors of earth indulge in aesthetic decadence, and where all the natural elements are within their power and avail-

able for mutation into whatever takes their fashionable fancy. The characters sport names such as Iron Orchid, The Duke of Queens, Brannart Morphail and Catherine Lilly Marguerite Natasha Dolores Beatrice Machineshop-seven Flambeau Gratitude. These inhabitants, empowered by strange rings, can create anything, distorting matter for their own enjoyment in a consistently metamorphosing world; they are bored necromancers, concerning themselves with the pursuit of their idiosyncratic fetishes and exuberances. Could this be an approximation of life in the near future, in an arena of playful but nihilistic gratuitousness? While this may seem extreme, bear in mind that a time when we possess the ability to live major parts of our lives in virtual futures may not be that far off. Currently, the technology is primitive, limited as we are to the clunky prosthetics of the head-mounted display and the data glove, but we must remember that the transition from the friction-and-gravity grip of the LP to the chromed rainbow of the laser compact disc was quick, and the light-

ion and its effective retrieval. One of the ways this can be done is through the invention of 'holons'.[1] The evolving art or science of holonics is influenced by Chaos Theory and Fractal Geometry. It makes particular use of the concept of 'self-sameness' or 'shelling', akin to what architects call 'scaling'. This 'running of a design up the scales' – so that it works on many levels and has a common formal quality at all scales – is much like the Apple icon system. From a simple basic unit, a complexity of information 'stores' can be generated that are easily understandable. Further, a hybrid holon and architectural 'structure' might be the key to person-

1 M Benedikt (ed.), *Cyberspace: The First Steps*, MIT Press, 1991 (particularly 'Notes on the Structure of Cyberspace' by Tim McFadden).

 alise and make 'friendly' data banks. Once a holon has been developed, it can be used to locate various scales of information (within a slide collection, for example, it could differentiate between years, trips, slide films, individual slides, bits of slides, bits of bits of slides, and so on). Its multidimensional spaces are ideally suited to architectural concerns such as circulation, order, form and symbol.

ning strike of technology will punctuate our lives evermore frequently.

Defying the Logic of Alphabets

Is there a case for the rejuvenation of the decrepit old architect into a hip, 'skull spark joker', a master of illusion?[3] Ironically, the architectural profession, now that it is banished to the ivory towers of academia and replaced on construction sites in the 'real' world by sycophantic, dribbling automata, could well make important contributions to the evolving topology and mapping of the virtually real worlds of cyberspace. To make significant inroads into this digital domain, architects must come to terms with the fact that much of their spatial understanding will be useless and that they must learn new notations and tactics of space forming. Such changes will not only change the role of the architect, but make architects of us all. The overriding architectural concerns will not be water tightness, gravity or human scale, but what it means to be 'human' or 'real'. Will virtual reality be of use in designing 'real' buildings? Yes, but only as an aid to visualisation, and not of much use when making interventions in deep cyberspace. The importation of existing gravity-bound structures and concepts into cyberspace denotes a lack of understanding about the possible nature of the cyberzone. Architecture will need to be fluid,[4] event-based, user-moulded and 'unsitely'.

Information will be the currency of cyberspace, psychology its physics; and its spaces will be shelled, folded, creased and wrinkled.[5] The stor-

3 The expression 'skull spark joker', lifted from Zodiac Mindwarp's song of the same name, is used to mean a mental magician. Whether Mr Mindwarp uses it in the same sense is unclear.

4 In 'The First Steps' chapter of *Cyberspace*, Marcos Novak considers Liquid Architecture.

5 Space may be folded or wrinkled many times in cyberspace.

this is an
information
house

an encryption method Information is power. The protection of cyberspace's per

age of information and how it is viewed will mould cyberspace and create a topology similar to that of a multidimensional city, reacting in time, space and perception to each individual user – a truly post-modern geography. In cyberspace, spatial archaeology will be commonplace. The flitting of sensation into the rich historical mix of the 'cybercity' will pass without comment as the nomadic user chooses to occupy spaces unparallel to 'real time'. And the alphabet of architecture will lose its vowels when the visible connection of spaces ceases to exist. In cyberspace there will be no need to incorporate traditional architectural devices such as corridors, for the journey from one space to another will not be linked to distance; it will merely cross a fold in the cyberspatial topology.

The Evolution of the Holy Goat

Iconography and semiotics will be deeply knitted into the new language of cyberspace. It is the space of lexical hybrids: simcit, cyberdelic, datacloud and teledildonics, to name just a few examples. This new information space with its internal and external interconnectedness is described by expressions such as the 'net' or the 'web' or the 'matrix', with the net currently being the most common. The net's construction is not based on Cartesian logic; its geometries reside in higher spatial dimensions.

In years to come the postman will never knock again, although we will continue to subcontract essential communication services to his digital descendants. Changes in postal systems are already occurring, with more adept computer users now owning semi-smart agent programs to sort, edit and reject mail of various configurations. But the implications of

d corporate information banks will be paramount. How is this to be achieved in a world where information towers are wholly visible and where computer hackers will be able to access cyberspace? Gibson and others have called the encryption systems in cyberspace ICE.[2] We already have ICE in the world with which we are familiar – locks on doors, passive infrared detectors, CCTV and so on – but these typologies of security will be ineffective and too primitive for use in cyberspace. 'Shadow', a useful tactic for cyberspace encryption, could be an effective guardian of data banks (in a system employing complex 'passforms' instead of passwords). Again, the

2 In the 'thanks' section of *Neuromancer*, Gibson gives credit for the invention of ICE to Tom Maddox, a fellow science-fiction writer.

cyberspatial innovation force us to assess ramifications of far more import than the demise of the postman. Here it is relevant to reflect on man's reflection. We will have the ability to be cyber Dorian Greys, concurrently many 'paintings' and selves. This technology could fulfil two of man's longest-held aspirations: ageless beauty and indestructibility. The baton of wish-fulfilment will be handed on from the makers of movies to the architects of cyberspace, whoever they might be. For the first time man will be able to crawl inside his most powerful construction, and this trek across the threshold between the real and the unreal will allow him not only to inhabit unimaginable spaces but change his reflection, both physically and metaphorically. In a future environment where perceptions can be choreographed in time and space, any digital form can take on associations personal to the viewer. In human terms, the traveller in cyberspace can choose to adopt any desired representation. The anthropocentric scale of the human frame is merely a menu option in these digitised terrains. Man may be represented as a goat or a collection of disparate, jumbled aggregations of machine parts – or anything (the semiotics of cyberspace will be complex and fluid). Perceptual relativity will be augmented and finely tuned by the user to create personal environments.

In Gibson's trilogy, cyberspace is populated not only by human agents but also by artificial intelligences (AIs). In *Neuromancer*, the nearly omnipresent AI Wintermute seems to be all-knowing and all-manipulating, achieving the status of a deity. By the time of *Mona Lisa Overdrive* (fourteen years further on in the narrative), Wintermute has been superseded by numerous polytheistic deities which are likened to the voodoo *loas*.

architect is uniquely qualified to generate such forms. Shadow has always been an architectural concern, although normally it is something that is discussed only vaguely and naïvely. To cast areas of sensitive information in shadow not only contributes to the problem of identification but also indicates that ICE is present. Shadow is one of the few elements that the cyberspace information 'city' will lack and is, therefore, a useful device. But what does the shadow conceal? What complex machinations occur in the split second upon entry into shadow space (s-space)? It seems that the 'key' is the production of formal icons/logos (call them what you

will) which join, split, flex or march in certain complex patterns – generated by genetic algorithms, perhaps, or the result of personal aesthetic choice. These icons could interact with other icons to determine entry to various levels of information, with the exact integration of disparate complex forms providing a readable, complex 'key'. The forms shown here illustrate the almost limitless formal lexicon that could be generated by any user as passforms. The complexity of any form is obviously dependent on the user's available computing power. Memory is paramount: the bigger the memory, the bigger the key.

digital

the life-box Cyberspace can also offer sanctuary to the dead. It is theoretically pos

'When the moment came, the bright time, there was absolute unity, one consciousness. But there was the other.'

'The other?'

'I speak only of that which I have known. Only the one has known the other, and the one is no more. In the wake of that knowing, the centre failed, every fragment rushed away. The fragments sought form, each one, as is the nature of things. In all the signs your kind have stored against the night, in that situation the paradigms of vodou proved most appropriate.' 6

6 William
Gibson,
Mona Lisa Overdrive.

Will the information highway become the voodoo highway? The deification of cyberspace is one of the more interesting possible manifestations of this technology. The net has encouraged many existing religious organisations to create their own 'home pages' and 'web sites'. Other religious groups are newly formed, to some extent as a result of certain aspects of the unique net environment. All manner of net pagans populate some of the far 'corners' of the Internet. As full bodily immersion in cyberspaces becomes more common, and cheaper, access to various hierarchies of information space may involve strange rites of passage.

This significant evolutionary step – that of virtually inhabiting cyberspace – creates a transhuman condition where it is possible to escape our frail, mushy, non-responsive, decaying, wet bodies for certain periods of time, the length of which will be dependent on technologies yet to be marketed. The full consequences of this are too complex to express without gross over-simplification, for it encompasses a considerable variety of socio-economic and cultural factors. But we may not be alone in these new landscapes, although artificial or machine intelligences will employ different criteria for the use and occupation of this spectacular unreality. Our navigation and

digital dreams

nd within fifty years may well be practically possible) to download human personality into cyberspace. If this occurs we will be witnesses to the emergence of immortality, resurrection and the complete death of 'real' time.

This introduces the notion of the life-box. A short story illustrates my point:

I returned home, the window was open.
Grandfather was jingling again.
I smiled at him, his red eye blinked back.
He was where I'd left him.
As he always was, hanging from the ceiling in the corner of the lounge.

I had a question to ask him.
I stood on a chair.
So he could look into my eyes.
He said 'Dave, good morning.'
I said 'Who made you? I mean, what I see.'
'I did, with the help of two architects.'
'How long have you been dead?'
'Fifty years,' came the reply.
'It's not so bad,' he giggled.
'I don't know I'm born.'

Imagine the sensation of being able to engage in conversation with a dead relative, a politician – or someone far more boring like an architect.

The life-box will contain the essence of grandad, an AI masquerading as grandad,

construction of cyberspace will seem slow and inert to the hyperreal machine – if it bothers to think about it at all. As cyberspace evolves it will 'peek' more and more into the 'real' world. It will slowly become omnipresent: we will be in the gaze of an unblinking electronic eye that is more powerful and discriminating than the ubiquitous closed-circuit TV camera of today. Cyberspace will be schizophrenic, with artificial intelligences appearing in numerous guises, determined by either themselves or the viewer; and machine perception will become as valid as human perception. Is man already beginning to create God by sculpting electrons? Is cyberspace to be a god of the future? It certainly has all the qualifications for deity status. But, as we shall see, it is not the only technology with the potential to snatch the mantle of the demiurge.

Dude Looks Like a Lady
In this new Eden after Apple, the form/function partnership that has been the fulcrum of architecture for the past one hundred years finds its last battle lost. The 'form follows function' mantra has finally been superseded. With technologies such as body mapping, it is possible to 'scan' into cyberspace three-dimensional representational images and, further, it is possible to morph, mutate and hybridise them. This makes the issues of copyright and encryption evermore important. But how do you legislate in the cyberzone? Where does the law stand when it has no firm ground on which to locate itself?

In cyberspace it will be possible to be someone else. There are many stories already, even in these early days, of people using the technology to extort, lie and even virtually rape others. In this sim-world we could all be cybercurators and collect menageries of bodies (not all human) as we currently collect

responding to questions in grandad's idiom.

The life-box could hang in the corner of a room, its carcass consisting of an aggregation of objects special to grandad: an old slipper (dangling from beneath perhaps), a wristwatch, a snuff box, or whatever might be significant to lives of the future – possibly to our own lives even (we could be the first grandads in the box).

Other motifs on the box might include fractal diagrams, for it has been postulated by some mathematicians and philosophers that life itself is fractal.3 As I sat down to write this with a green pen, I wondered about my hand-writing: memories of school, of learning to write, the smell of the oil boiler in the classroom. A fractal map could be drawn of these complex interrelationships and, if the system were hugely elaborated, of a whole life.

It may be a concern for many in the future to endeavour to

3 R Rucker, *Mind Tools*, Houghton Mifflin, 1987.

record as much as they can of their fractal lives. Indeed, as Rudy Rucker postulates, the person who invents a working life-box will become very rich.

Further into the future, but maybe in parallel with the manifestations of the physical life-box, the cyberspace life-box might sail like a ghostly ark, unrestrained, through cyberspace information walls and shadow. A soul Tardis.

With the emergent science of body mapping, in cyberspace it may be possible to meet grandad in person (aged whatever you want), have dinner with Winston Churchill, be present when Newton felt the bump on his head, or keep company with Hendrix on that fateful night.

The issue of body and personality copyright is crucial. How will we choose who is to mind our mind? Will the entertainment aspect of cyberspace transcend into a full epistemological shift, or is it destined to slumber in the amusement arcade where Gibson found it?

Con 1 Alan Turing, visionary genius and founding father of artificial intelligence (AI), saw no reason why an artificially intelli

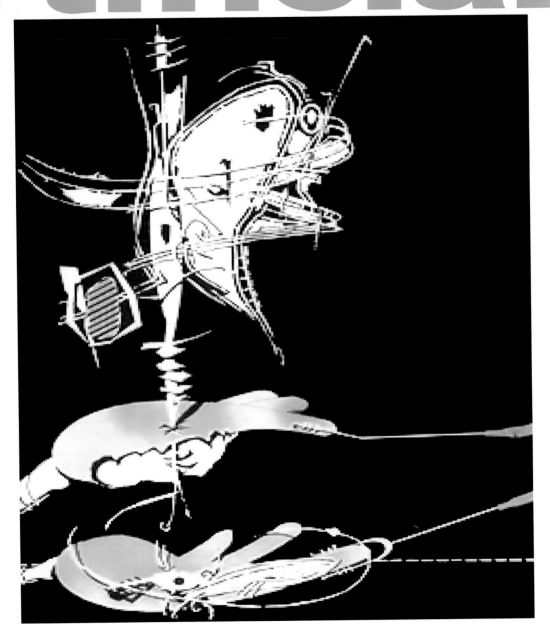

56

e could not be created by the year 2000. Now, with the benefit of being further along the trajectory of Time's Arrow, it seems unlikely that this critical evolutionary step will be taken during the remnants of this century. But, bearing in mind that the computing power of the little plastic box in your briefcase doubles every fourteen months or so, it must surely happen in the next millennium. The fate of the flesh Luddites will be the same as that of their namesakes from an earlier industrial age, with their biochauvinism seen as quaint and romantic (but ultimately anachronistic) in a universe teeming with lifeforms that are either non-biological or only partially so.

Turing developed a simple test to ascertain whether a machine possesses AI. A human communicates with an unseen entity in another room. If this entity turns out to be a machine, provided it gives convincing human replies to any question that the human decides to ask, it passes the Turing Test. (It would seem that Turing valued the ability of such a machine to lie! But that is by the by.) Once the Turing Test is passed and artificial intelligence is born,

shirts – ready to slip into when they suit us. With software becoming increasingly cheap and accurate, might vagueness soon be at a premium, and non-specificness a status symbol? It can't be long before cyberspace is populated by pollen clouds, coldness or the smell of grilled steak and other sensory stimuli. All these possible combinations create a magical space where humanity can potentially leave the nadir of mobility that has characterised its useful yet ultimately limited symbiosis with the meat packing of the body.

Love is Automatic Pleasure

Our real world interaction is in part conducted through other members of society with whom we share an empathy. Psychologists call these people 'significant others', with the significance being familial or romantic. Many believe our psychological wellbeing is dependent on these others, but the debate about the influence on our personalities of both genetics and behaviour (and their interaction) is far from finished. What of a psychological profile where the significant other is a chameleon-like, non-placed and electronic entity? What effects could such phenomena have on our psychology? What will happen when the 'real' world becomes a place that we inhabit when our cyberprosthetics are taken away from us – a world of turgid greys and murky inertia, a type of treacle-space where movement and perception are difficult? The street would become worldwide, a place that is cold, wet, polluted and invisible to the majority of humanity, a space left over after scanning. We are creating a new plastic medium: cyberplasm, the progeny of the electron. One hundred years after the discovery of the electron, this seems appropriate. The ubiquity of the electron has created the ubiquity of information,

the world will surely stop and ponder briefly while Genesis is rewound and prepared to go forward again. Cyborg Man will have created the Electric Ape, but not in his own image. The second coming will not involve the spilling of blood, only bits and pieces will be sacrificed.

Con 1 is intended to be an instantly recognisable icon – and it will be! Once the prophets of doom and cybersoothsayers adopt it for future postulates on AI, this icon will become manifest – by a simple algorithm in or on any known information medium – the moment the Turing Test is passed. It will be thrust on to TV programmes, appear miraculously as obstacles in virtual reality terrains, be thrown on to the front pages of newspapers, infest home pages on the Internet, be the postmark of the day on snail mail (traditional postal systems), and feature in many other applications. Like any multimedia experience of the future, icons will be moulded to individual preoccupations and concerns.

Con 2 Areas of cyberspatial terrain inhabited by AIs, fleetingly or otherwise, will perhaps be akin to roadworks on the super

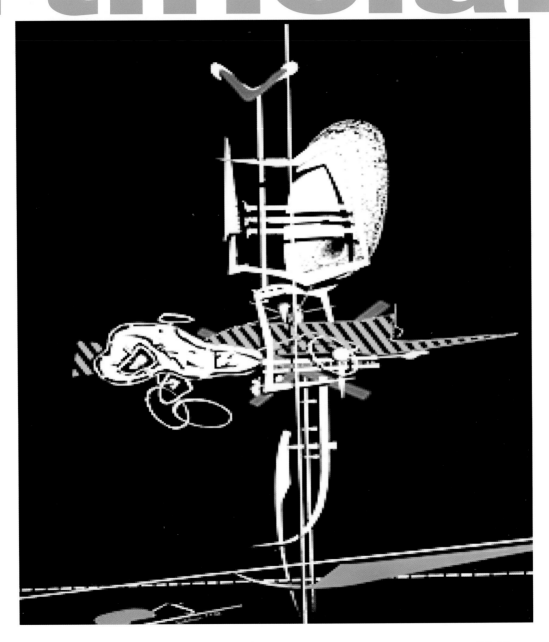

digital dreams

warning icon will be required. Again, it must be clearly recognisable in order to deter the casual cyberjock from entering areas of unlimited headroom. Why would we use the expression 'headroom'? Because AIs will occupy a higher order of multidimensional space, one that the human, wet mind would not be able to comprehend, or even maintain sanity within. Such spaces would decompose and reconfigure millions, maybe billions, of times a second. Even augmented human intelligences will have little chance in such cyber black holes. This icon will indeed be the sign of the 'other', the digitised thinking-machine presence. AI is the final gift we have to share. It will have a high price, but we have no choice but to pay. We shall never be alone in the universe again.

place and sense. In the no man's land of binary bits, all that is needed is the correct transceiving device.

To many this may seem a despotic, chaotic world, a nightmare scenario with gaping philosophical problems; but to others it may seem the ultimate Utopian space. Obviously the uses and abuses of cyberspace are potentially huge and are only now starting to be explored and quantified. Fully immersible cyberspace *will* happen, and be available at a store near you soon. We cannot disinvent the concept. We must learn how to control cyberspace and allow it to be accessible to society as a whole. Those who see cyberspace purely as some sort of recreational or commercial space with little impact on the 'real' world are wrong. They fail to comprehend the far-reaching effects this technology will have on our societies and communities by extending the sphere of influence of our bodies. While holidaying in Digitland is always an option, the effects on the human psyche are potentially devastating – or liberating, depending on your point of view.7

We have crossed the Technicon! And there's no point in looking back.

7 The point of view (POV) is crucial to any evaluation, navigation or experience in cyberspace; a type of visual relativity pervades cyberspace and any discussion of it.

shape-shifting in technical ecstasy

Now that some of the general concepts and issues which cyberspace engenders have been introduced, it is important to explore ideas of dislocation and ecstasy. These notions are crucial to some of the architectures and processes that will be considered later.

Could it be that cyberspace is the culmination of man's search for a 'bridge to heaven', a search that has encompassed the use of narcotics, ritual and meditation, all of which are the foundation of a variety of ecstatic religions? The continuing quest for experiences of the realm of the gods has normally involved the use of intermediaries, such as prophets, angels, demons, chimeras, familiars and shamans. This chapter explores the nature of shamanistic practices as a way of describing some of the more incredible potentials of cyberspace.

To describe cyberspace as an ecstatic space leads us to two at first seemingly discrete readings of these potentials. The etymology of the Greek *ecstasis*[1] is concerned with the notion of disjuncture: to be beside yourself, out of your face or not full of your skin; that is, to occupy a non-body-centric space. This derangement of the body and 'soul' is an escape from their usual earthly relationship. The dislocation of body and soul encourages a perceptually different order of experience, a readjustment of the normal mental and visual perceptual parallax.

The ecstatic religions, such as those of the native North Americans, utilise a shaman (a witchdoctor or medicine man). This mediator, a messenger between earth and culturally important spiritual terrains, is able to inform

I enter the fireplace and quickly shoot up the chimney into a lightish grey, whirling cloud tunnel. Soon I'm aware of my guardian – a pelican with a pink beak … As we draw closer I see that, built on the top of the mountain, is a magnificent palace made of golden crystal, radiating lime-yellow light. I am told this is the palace of the phoenix, and I then see that golden bird surmounting the edifice. It seems to be connected with my own power-hawk.

Notes of a shamanistic trip, Nevill Drury, *The Elements of Shamanism*

Inner eye opening to the stepped pyramid of the Eastern Seaboard Fission Authority burning beyond the green cubes of Mitsubishi Bank of America, and high and very far away he saw the spiral arms of military systems, forever beyond his reach. And somewhere he was laughing, in a white painted loft, distant fingers caressing the deck, tears of release streaking his face.

William Gibson, *Neuromancer*

1 D Goldblatt, 'The Dislocation of the Architectural Self', *The Journal of Aesthetics and Art Criticism*, 49:4, 1991. This article explains the notion of ecstasy as a device of art and architecture for escaping the formalist nature of the artistic self.

the other members of his community about the nature of the gods.

In the art world, ecstatic concepts have been likened to processes that attempt to dislocate the artist from the product; they have been called the second aesthetic – the aesthetic of the algorithm, the rules of problem solving. (The first aesthetic is that of form giving, as in traditional architectural practice). The second aesthetic's beauty, independent of input and product, is based on methods of solution or dissolution.

It seems that the concern of the architects of cyberspace should be the second aesthetic – the 'if/then' binary logic of the algorithm. The first aesthetic will look after itself. In one sense this is the philosophy of enabling, but not the enabling of anything, anywhere, anytime; it is, rather, a philosophy of enabling that is not concerned with the omnipresent and benevolent jacket of Beaubourg. It is a notion of enabling where it is difficult to postulate final physical form, geographical parameters and exact placements: an ill-defined transience of codification and interaction of objects, an architecture and semiology out of aesthetic control.

These two aspects of the interpretation of ecstasy, that of shamanism and process (the methods of solution and dissolution), when used in relation to cyberspace are not, however, mutually exclusive.

Jacking Up and Jacking In

Cyberspace has demiurgical status, it breathes life into the inanimate and it has innate knowledge of various agents' intentions and physical make-up. To travel to the 'other side' the shaman utilises a vehicle (often a drum beat) which is seen as a type of shamanistic horse. (Strangely, using heroin is

zero

Woolwich, south London, is a typical Victorian urban area. Its function has been made anachronistic by changes in technology and political emphasis. Woolwich was once a centre for military personnel and the manufacture of military equipment (in recognition of this fact, its railway station is called Woolwich Arsenal). As the eye of the technological hurricane has repositioned itself over the years, Woolwich has become more detached from these invigorating effects. It could be said that the overriding problem for Woolwich is one of location: Woolwich should really be in Silicon Valley. Therefore, Woolwich's sheer physicality and its inherent inertia are the genesis of its problem. This physicality is in part a consequence of using historically stupid materials whose inertness and lack of mobility are nothing short of murderous. These materials kill any attempt to revitalise the ailing town. The fact is that in the 1990s Woolwich is badly aimed, and this is the fundamental issue that any plans for economic rejuvenation must deal with.

Within this context, architecture is of little use. Minor, strategic additions can ameliorate only minor issues of urban connectedness. The big question should be: how might we centralise Woolwich in the economy of the future? The

2 The Almighty, 'Joy Bang One Time Soul Destruction', Polydor, 1991.

referred to by addicts as 'doing horse'.[2]) The beat of the drum is a concentrational tactic that facilitates the shaman's slow disentanglement from the mundanity of earthly concerns and experiences. This process is augmented by the use of various hallucinogens: tobacco, Morning Glory, mushrooms and, in the case of the South American shaman, *Banisteriopsis caapi* – the vine of the soul. These plants take on a special place in ecstatic mythologies, and are made sacred for the power of the experience they provide. Similarly, Case, the anti-hero in Gibson's *Neuromancer*, has a hi-tech equivalent to the drum/stallion and is addicted to the thrill of the ecstatic cyberspace experience. Interestingly, the name Case implies a container, a hollow repository waiting to be filled, animated or enlivened. Case 'rides' the cyberdeck and achieves a dislocation of self through prosthetic 'dermatrodes' strapped to his forehead.[3] Case is the hi-tech shaman reincarnated as a virtual addict or prostitute of the twenty-first century. '"It's like I'm using," Case heard someone say … "It's like my body's developed this massive drug deficiency."'[4]

3 Numerous prosthetic devices for cyberspatial access have been postulated: 'trodes, jacks, etc.

4 W Gibson, *Neuromancer*, p.9.

Like Case, the shaman is active as opposed to passive in his trance-induced 'realities'. Once at the threshold of the celestial realm, the shaman is given, or finds, a spirit guide, a dead relative or a familiar animal – a bird or a bear. Often this guardian spirit is identified as the psychic counterpart of the shaman. (There is another analogy here with the alchemist and his mystic sister.) For example, the spirit guide of a traditional shaman who would summon named spirits by inserting different pebbles into a gourd was often a hawk. Even now a fully fledged cybershaman has the ability to determine his own familiar guardian or to summon

digital dreams

answer questions the nature of place, reality and death. These larger philosophical ideas are inherently architectural. Masterplans must not confine themselves to 'real' space; they must explore unreal spaces also.

Architecture as we know it, is to a large extent influenced by the current scale of our bodies. In the future this scale will not remain consistent. It has been argued that the human race is on the edge of an evolutionary discontinuity which will manifest itself as the emergence of *Homo comboticus* (a hybrid human/computer/robot). It could be said that there is no point in arguing about the integrity of the bag of carbon and water we call our bodies, or the three pounds of grey mush we call our minds. The world is changing so quickly, our perceptions flitting from real to unreal so fast, that our naïve conception of reality means nothing.

Woolwich should buy 'real virtual freehold' or 'unreal real estate'. It should invest in memory – not heritage-centred memory but RAM – and learn a lesson from its more attractive neighbour, Greenwich. Because Greenwich is a point of access into our system of time keeping, it consequently has world significance for astronomers and laymen alike. Woolwich could be the 'gateway' to our conception of cyberspace, 'the space that is no place'. Navigation through the topology of the 'world virtual city' will need to be dependent on a static point of entry to ensure a

known but unreal guides from a growing and complex virtual cosmology of agents, demons and gophers. This software-surrogates trend will continue as more and more menial – and not so menial – tasks are required in an information-rich hyperlinked world. In Iain Banks' *Feersum Endjinn*,5 characters sometimes meet previous versions of themselves to help them navigate the hierarchies of the virtual realities of Banks' cyberspace: the crypt. The guardian spirit can even be a previous self! These guardians of various domains might also be AI-originated, or they might be policing expert systems. There could be a hierarchy of cybershamans, as there is for normal shamans. The human cybershaman, however, unlike his AI cousin, will not be able to travel into the higher levels of cyberspace – and anyway, these higher domains would make little sense to a meat-originated intelligence.

5 I Banks, *Feersum Endjinn*, Orbit, 1994. Banks also uses hawks as guardians of the crypt. His chimeras are called 'lammergeiers'.

Shamans usually enter a type of tunnel at the beginning of their journey – a tube to the other, celestial world. Gibson paraphrases this tunnel as an architecture of possibility: 'And in the bloodlit dark behind his eyes, silver phosphenes boiling in from the edge of space, hypnagogic images jerking past like film compiled from random frames. Symbols, figures, faces, a blurred fragmented mandala of visual information. Please, he prayed. Now.'6 The tunnel he describes is an extruded mandala in fractally bifurcating hypervisual splendour: a cybergate. Such gates are points of entry into specific cyberspatial environments, where quick orientation and a swift understanding of the navigational and informational possibilities are required by the new user. These 'places' are essentially cyberspatial signposts.

6 Gibson, op. cit. p. 68.

digital dreams

quick, effective orientation for the new arrival. This point could be Virtual Woolwich. This simulated Woolwich would bear little resemblance to the London Woolwich; it would merely be the compulsory point of access to cyberspace, an information corridor (similar to an air corridor). Revenue for entering cyberspace would be paid to Woolwich by all worldwide users of the future virtual reality net (in the same way that one pays for telephone services). The revenue would be massive and Woolwich's real urban problems would be solved. The zone between the real and the unreal is the most interesting area. A proposition such as this provides opportunities for the virtual to flow into the real across blurred boundaries.

The major element of the proposal is, therefore, the cybergate – the virtual and vital linkage that appears in real space as a necessary, urban link from the old Arsenal site to the bottom of Powis Street (Woolwich's main street). In virtual

Reality Janitors and Cyberwizards

Cyberspace is not only a space travelled to in ecstatic derangement; it is intrinsically an ecstatic space, dependent on a series of interrelated hierarchies of algorithms – but sometimes not. The deranged arrangement of cyberspace can encourage synchronicity; programs already exist that facilitate the serendipitous. One such program is Textmangler, which reorganises text using a series of grammatical rules manifested by an algorithm: the chance encounter of text could be the precursor of personality or reality mangling, chance meetings, or linkages and alliances in an unstable terrain. Genetic algorithms may further morph these spaces through a series of evolutionary mutations. The good, the bad and the ugly may only be manifestations of the same space or object along its evolutionary trajectory. 'Enigma' might become the subtext of cyberspace, with AIs taking the role of angels and prophets, transforming, pointing and advising on the uses and the navigation of the fluxing topology of the celestial architecture of cyberspace, in a series of revelatory experiences for the cybernaut. The city of cyberspace will be beside itself, ecstatically deranged; in real cities, agents, some smart, some not, will be required to order and edit other aspects of 'reality'. Shamans will also be needed on this side of the computer interface to instruct the virgin user of cyberspace in the techniques and protocols of 'surfing'. As the bandwidth of cyberspace increases, so too does the complexity of creating and interacting with responsive virtual environments.

'Spamming' the Meat Puppet

Once the cybernaut can hunt in cyberspace, it will be important to consider the obverse of this situation. Will it be possi-

1 There are numerous reasons why cyberspace might want to mimic the real topology of cities. This would, for example, aid navigation and posit a ground plane. However, what is at issue is how similar the two might be. Many factors are different – in cyberspace speed of travel is much faster, and collisions with cybersubstance would have different consequences, for instance – so their similarity would be limited. An interesting cyberspace scenario is Neal Stephenson's concept of the Metaverse in his novel *Snowcrash* (Roc, Penguin Books, 1993). Along the great length of its main constituent, 'The Street', are the cyberspatial headquarters of various corporations, including a communal space for hackers. These spaces are populated by avatars of real users and software daemons. One particular type of daemon, the Graveyard Daemon, acts out a cyberburial ritual and carries off avatars that have been dismembered for funeral rites after virtual dismemberment has occurred. This inhibits the real-world user for a period of time until the ritual is complete.

ble for cyberspace, or perhaps some of its unholy horde, to travel in the opposite direction, down an electronic conduit controlling elements of personal, mental and physical real space? The machine hunter from the nowhere heavens could make you its prey. This idea – that the physical body could be a space of possession – is echoed in the voodoo of Haiti, 'where the "Divine Horsemen" or *loa* divinities, are said to descend upon the trance subjects during their ecstatic rituals and "ride" them in a frenzy.'[7] The control of the 'others' by the use of electronic pads and electric currents – to muscles which then react, either violently or not, depending on their voltage – has been achievable for some time. These primitive first steps introduce us to another aspect of the dissolution of self: the philosophical and ethical problems that arise when someone or something takes over someone else's meat puppet (the body, the moist blood highway that hangs below your hair!). 'Spamming', a process of invading a fellow net user's screen and flooding it with incoherent rubbish (named after the famous Monty Python sketch about Spam), is already well known. This takes on serious implications if the meat puppet itself can be spammed – personality could be erased, augmented, juxtaposed, stolen or hidden behind – and presumably there would be attempts to make such activities illegal. Spamming could perhaps result in epilepsy if someone or something were to spam the wetware of someone's personal neural net. The identity of self becomes as potentially fragmented a concept as the schizophrenic's personality. Interestingly, epilepsy and schizophrenia are seen by shamanistic cultures as manifestations of the presence of the spiritual world. Indeed, if you accept the thesis that cyberspace has

7 N Drury, *The Elements of Shamanism*, Element Books, 1989, pp. 11–12.

space it would appear as a pulsating navigational device and nightclub, where virtual assignations are acted out and viewed in real space by travellers on the real link. Opportunities to 'jack in' and join the virtual throng will be provided for the 'high bandwidth surfer'.[1]

It is here that we must consider the issue of consciousness and the evolution of digital minds. Part of this is the possible downloading of human minds into cybercit to escape the body's 'meat' death. Once downloading of human consciousness occurs, communication conduits to the real world become important – so that the virtual can interact directly with the real. The old Arsenal site (already a graveyard of sorts) would become a graveyard for all downloaded consciousnesses. Thanks to the ubiquitous cathode ray tube, gravestones would be capable of receiving graven images, messages from beyond the grave, edited and projected by the individual silicon intelligence concerned.

The founding fathers of virtual Woolwich will provide a 'starter pack' for future formal connection. These genes of form (a package of formal possibility) will be the raw material for the virtual architecture immediately around the cybergate. Some of these components will be

8 P Cadigan, *Fools*, Bantam Spectra, 1992. In one sense Cadigan's text mimics and augments our existing schizophrenic reality; the self becomes a series of actors, each appropriate for different situations, each unsure who 'me' is because of interference from the others.

the potential to assume deity status, 'spamming the meat puppet' would be akin to the act normally accorded the gods – the ability to 'strike down' wrong-doers or heretics.

In Pat Cadigan's novel *Fools*,[8] the Brain Police adopt personalities to destabilise a criminal fraternity of mind-suckers and body-snatchers, where personalities are for sale. Will cyberspace exorcisms need to be medically conducted, not with invasive surgery but by booting-up back-up copies of saved memic software to run on erased virtual machine wetware? We might in the not-so-distant future need to 'save' ourselves every now and again, and this would be good mental management.

Excommunication and the Toad

The cybernaut's biggest fear must be the truncation of his cyberprivileges: the data stroke or a byte attack. Cybersinners have many advantages over their unaltered earthbound egos; they can commit their crimes in a faceless, nameless and bodiless state so that their subsequent apprehension ('the accused was proceeding in a multidimensional direction') would be hugely difficult. The excommunication of cybersinners, whatever their offence – currently virtual rape and hacking (ICE breaking), but later perhaps also mind-sucking, live body-snatching, meat-spamming and eye-surfing – is called 'toading'. This is the effective banishment of the sinner to the real nether world, condemned for ever to reside in the fires of the hellishly real. For the would-be cryptographic cardinals of cyberspace, control of any sort will be an uphill battle.

digital dreams

morphed into a virtual university department which will concern itself with genetic and silicon intelligence, biomemetics, virtuality and consciousness. This terrain will be the virtual meeting ground for the world's leading scientists in these disciplines.

Woolwich will become virtually central and globally famous. To become unreal is Woolwich's only real chance!

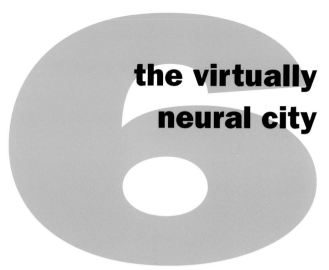

the virtually neural city

... like any organism [a city] has a circulatory system in its streets, railroads and rivers, a brain in its universities and planning offices, a digestive system in its food distribution and sewage lines, muscles in its industrial centres, and any city worthy of the name has an erogenous zone...

Matthew Dumont, *Arthropods*, London, 1971.

Historically, the city has been seen as either mechanistic or biological in its order. This 'hive' or 'timepiece' approach is essentially reductive, whichever side of the duality is pursued. The city can also be seen as the product of the invisible, the virtual – a complex mesh of interacting nodes which operate at a variety of scales simultaneously. Researches in what we call 'virtuality theory'[1] are forcing urban planners to accept the role of the invisible through the recognition of the symptoms of space-time compaction and information ubiquity. This interconnectedness will cause the nodal nature of the city to be further dispersed (the accelerating complexity of the city has always been part product of the virtual). This virtual aspect of the city is becoming more and more important as a definable component of human habitation.

In recent years, classical science's mechanistic explanations of matter and its motion, while holding near-enough true not to upset our everyday 'naïve' reality, have been attacked for their insistent linearity. These linear theories predict that all systems are subject to an understandable order and a conditioned repetition. However, some scientists are coming to believe that complex systems such as human societies, the weather, ecosystems and the mind, are non-linear. Non-linear systems have two main characteristics: they are not predictable, and any small fluctuations that may exist within the network are capable of causing huge fluctuations in effect. Chaos theory is an example of the study of non-linear dynamics.[2] It seems that complex systems exhibit what physicists call 'phase transition'. This changes the nature of a system both drastically and quite abruptly, pushing it into another phase. An

1 'Virtuality theory' covers researches and philosophies in all types of virtuality, from communication to full cyberspace.

2 J Gleick's *Chaos* (Cardinal, 1988) is a must for anyone interested in fractal geometry and other chaotic phenomena.

example of this is the sudden transition from single-cell organisms to multi-celled creatures 600 million years ago, or the sudden change in the social organisation of a particular society during the course of its evolution. These 'phase transitions' are linked to the notion of 'strange attractors' in chaos theory. Strange attractors exist in systems that remain in a constant state until a significant fluctuation occurs that causes the whole system to change suddenly; it then settles into a state of equilibrium until the next significant disturbance. The evolution of solid-state computational power has enabled such systems to be mapped. Some of these algorithmically simple but complexly interacting systems are cellular automata. The simple rules of these systems quickly generate a series of complex relationships and these evolve over a number of generations on the computer screen.[3] Studies such as these have helped towards an understanding of a condition called 'the edge of chaos', a state which has a creative aspect in that it shows a sense of order. The idea that universal computing ability (as identified by Turing and von Neumann)[4] could be achieved in this state between order and chaos, was important to further theories concerning other complex systems, including biological evolution. The question that has been raised is: are all these systems being directed to the edge of chaos in pursuit of a maximum computational ability which will yield an advantage in the search for evolutionary fitness?

Further study of cellular automata has shown them to be influenced by 'emergent' behaviour. Emergent characteristics include a system's ability to evolve behavioural traits that were not originally programmed into

3 The invention of particular cellular automata and the 'Game of Life' are explained in more detail in the secondary text, 'Hair Between Lips'.

4 The postulation of the universal computing machine (Turing) and cellular automata theory (von Neumann) is documented in J D Bolter's *Turing's Men*, Penguin, 1993. For an introduction to the important work of Turing and von Neumann, see S Levy, *Artificial Life*, Penguin, 1992.

digital dreams

it. Emergence phenomena in cellular automata can generate the evolution of behavioural hierarchies, with automata progressing from single cells to multi-celled specialists and developing 'flock' characteristics.

It has been postulated that human societies can be seen as the result of biological attractors. Such attractors seem to exist in ant colonies, for example, and both ant and human societies can be seen as having emergent qualities. Communication is vital in the internal workings of any social grouping, including that of insects, and in human society the role of language cannot be over-stressed.

The issue of emergence has far-reaching consequences for any notion of complex systems and group dynamics. The complex system of the human mind might also be conditioned by emergent phenomena and this could give us an insight into consciousness itself. Daniel Dennett has said: 'Emergence is what my model [of consciousness] and their [the scientists exploring complexity] approaches have in common ... But, yes, emergence is a real hard science phenomenon and it is central to understanding consciousness.'[5] This suggests that the mind is a type of society; if this is the case, is its organisation mimicked in human societies? Are the workings of our minds visible to us simply by looking around us? Is there a mind of the city? Is the mind of the city an echo of the city of the mind?

5 R Lewin, *Complexity*, Phoenix, 1993, p. 157.

Of Demons, Agents and Little Men

As children, many of us imagine that inside our heads are little people who organise our every action and thought. Many concepts of the mind use this same analogy, to a greater or lesser extent, and are called 'homunculus' theories, but

6 The idea of the homunculus has been taken from alchemic texts. Jung sees the homunculus as an alchemic graphic code for the role of the 'infantile child' in the unconscious, but is otherwise vague about its full alchemic significance. The term homunculus is also used in neurobiology for contortions in the representation of the human body when it is mapped proportionally to accord with various criteria of human sensibility. The hands of the 'touch' homunculus, for instance, are larger than the upper arms.

researchers have replaced our simple childhood visions with various notions of modularity, agents and demons.6 These theories are dependent on assumptions as to whether or not there is a hierarchy within the complex interaction of these modules.

Some of the contemporary work in artificial intelligence is also dependent on the notion of homunculi (or units of competence) and, again, one of the fundamental issues is whether there is a predefined structure to the homuncular babble or whether it is anarchic. The 'lack of order' theories of the latter view are called 'pandemonium' theories. In Dennett's theory of consciousness he eloquently puts forward this concept, arguing that this pandemonium creates 'lots of duplication of effort, wasted motion, interference, periods of chaos and layabouts with no fixed job description'.7 Other manifestations of the homunculus theory include Marvin Minsky's 'agents'. In his book *The Society of the Mind*,8 he posits a complex series of interactions between various agents as the basis for consciousness. Each agent, very similar to a human participant in society, has inherited characteristics and certain skill specialisations. But, again, we must return to Dennett for a succinct description of this pandemonium and its lack of hierarchy:

7 D Dennett, *Consciousness Explained*, p. 261.

8 M Minsky, *The Society of the Mind*, Simon and Schuster, 1985.

9 Dennett, op. cit. p. 263.

They [the specialist demons] are often opportunistically enlisted in new roles, for which their native talents more or less suit them. The result is not bedlam only because the trends that are imposed on all this activity are themselves the product of design. Some of the design is innate, and is shared with other animals. But it is augmented, and sometimes even overwhelmed in importance, by micro habits of thought that are developed in the individual, partly idiosyncratic results of self-exploration and partly the predesigned gifts of culture. Thousands of memes, mostly borne by language, but also by wordless 'images' and other data structures, take up residence in an individual brain, shaping its tendencies and thereby turning it into a mind.9

It might be instructive, perhaps, to replace the words 'brain' and 'mind' with 'city' and 'society'.

The Emergence of Parallelism

If computer minds are to be able to simulate human thought or, indeed, be machine intelligences,[10] digital processing must become parallel to but away from the linear processing common to our personal computers. This parallelism could achieve the constant babble of the pandemonium of the homunculus theories. This type of processing would allow the simultaneous processing of disparate and sometimes contradictory data. Some scientists' faith in AI is based on the assumption that a drastic increase in computational power will in itself create artificial intelligence – as a result of the emergent criteria which will come into being as the system achieves greater complexity.

Parallel processing is behind the development of the powerful Connection Machine. Its creator, Danny Hillis, describes the machine as 'trivial in complexity compared with the brain of a fly'.[11] The Connection Machine has 65,536 parallel processors; the key to its working method is its ability to communicate among its parts, not unlike a telephone system. It is possible that in a future generation of the Connection Machine, intelligence may emerge. Theories in AI and brain sciences that use this type of thinking are called 'connectionist' theories. As Marvin Minsky has said, the human brain is 'a computer made of meat', with 10 billion neurons and 60,000 miles of 'wiring'. This massive connectedness undoubtedly has something to do

10 Harry Harrison and Marvin Minsky's *The Turing Option* (Penguin, 1993) is a science-fiction story of the invention of the first AI and the complex conspiracy of the subsequent industrial espionage. The AI 'Sven' insists on being called a machine intelligence, not an artificial intelligence. This brings in the notion of 'weak' and 'strong' AIs: 'weak' is human mimicry, 'strong' includes the ability of a machine intelligence to evolve 'mentally' at a faster rate than its human counterpart. Sven quickly becomes 'smarter' than his inventor, thanks to his faster processing power and the fact that he is in tune with many environmental inputs neither visible nor audible to humans.

11 Levy, op. cit. p. 160.

Hair between lips, they all return

to their roots, in a blinding fireball

I envisage their return, until he moves his fingers

slowly and, although things flourish,

takes on the well-known mushroom shape endeavouring

to grasp while the multitude of things

comes into being.

In the hearts of many academics, Cambridge has a special place, an almost mythical existence within academic space. Its hallowed halls have been host to some of the most innovative thinkers in history. This fact, combined with the city's more than fair share of architectural gems, has given Cambridge an enviable position on the world map.

Parker's Piece is a near-square of near-central green space. It is this quality of 'nearness' and the implication of 'almostness' that is its limitation ('nearness' needs to be converted into a quality dependent not on adjacency but on independency). Suddenly the quiet kid in the good school shows himself to be an interesting contributor to the debate.

Currently, Parker's Piece is not contributing to any debate; it stands quietly in the corner of the architectural playground, embarrassed and sullen. It is not special, it needs to be imbued with personality and purpose. We decide to address this overriding architectural and geographical problem.

The purpose of this intervention is to create a necessary architectural presence and provide a character for Parker's Piece that is different yet contextually specific. But a building on the corner site would not serve as a useful catalyst and would only solve micro-architectural concerns. Whatever the actual architectonics we propose, the result must drag the area out of the facelessness of the collegiate hinterland.

Historically, Cambridge has been the backdrop for many profound advances in theoretical endeavour.

with consciousness. For the connectionists the fundamental question is how do we/the machine adopt a strategy that results in a series of coherent thoughts? Is there a type of editing system, or a 'place' where everything can 'talk' to everything else? Can 'specialist' networks be called into use for non-specialist or generalist tasks? This flip between specialist and generalist function is mirrored in human interaction; we all adopt activities that we specialise in (architecture, for example) and others that we 'generalise' in (such as architectural journalism). Further, specialist data can be transferred across a system by generalising agents – this text, perhaps, is an example. The multivalent nature of neural agents (demons, call them what you will) has not yet been fully exploited in the realms of architecture and the city. But it is thought that the ongoing evolution of smart materials will go some way towards the realisation of an architecture that is multifunctioning, responsive and connected.

Other researchers in this field posit the notion of 'rapid modulators' that mediate between neurons or sets of neurons. These transient structures are swiftly assembled and disassembled. Again, the mediation of a transient infrastructure is not new to architectural theory, but the emphasis of this transience is concerned not with the module and its internal working (although this might also be true), but with a type of transient, organisational, 'global' infrastructure.

Mind the City
This brief synopsis of some of the constantly evolving theories of consciousness and AI might, perhaps, lead to a clearer understanding of the city and of the architecture within it, for there is a powerful analogy between the mind and the city. Is it

digital dreams

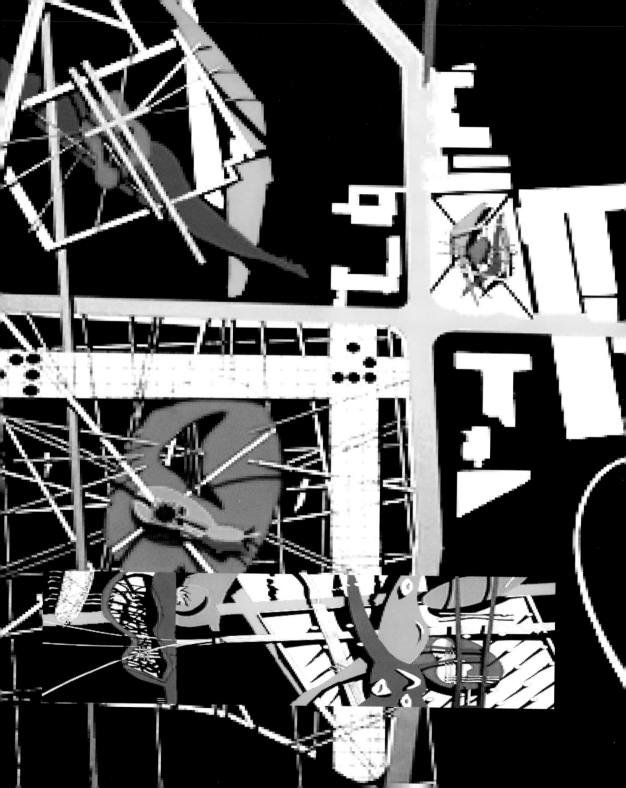

Some of these ideas have, or will have, a radical impact on our notions of place in relation to our surroundings, our technologies and our human neighbours. Perhaps, potentially, the greatest of these ideas are in the field of artificial intelligence. It was at Cambridge that fundamental breakthroughs in this research were made. These leaps forward have enabled our information age to flourish. Two researchers need to be specifically mentioned: Alan Turing and John Horton Conway; the former for his pioneering work on the conceptual automata (the Turing Machine) and his test for verifying AI (the Turing Test), the latter for his invention of the 'Game of Life'.

During the 1930s Turing's research led him to postulate, and to prove mathematically, the theoretical existence of a universal machine which could function as any other machine, given the right input. He went further by suggesting that the human mind was such a machine, and that it could also be duplicated by his theoretical engine. This was the genesis of artificial intelligence theory.

In the late 1960s John Horton Conway created a simple game that was to concur with John von Neumann's aspirations for cellular automata and their universal computing abilities. The game consisted of a few elementary rules and was acted out on an infinite Euclidean plane with tessellating squares – in effect, a massive chess board. Each square was a conceptual cell; each cell had the capacity to be alive or dead and was surrounded by eight other such cells. Once a cell became alive, its survival depended on the number of adjacent cells that were also alive. It would not survive if there were fewer than two others also alive, and it would die of claustrophobia if there were more than three neighbours alive. If a cell was dead, it could be reborn in the next generation if three surrounding cells had been alive in the previous generation. This was a universal computer, a cellular automaton. Over many generations, patterns emerged and were given names, 'glider' being one of the most important. A glider is a cell configuration that releases itself from the main body of the game and moves off into infinite space, progressing along and reforming its configuration over a series of generations. The glider can be used in conjunction with a 'glider-gun', a cellular form that can produce gliders at regular intervals. The interaction of the gliders with other cellular structures is the basis of their computational ability. Today this work is being further researched around the world. Some believe it to be the basis of natural life and a crucial step towards machine intelligence (via the phenomenon of emergence).

This is only a short introduction to the strange world of AI research, but the importance of this work cannot be over-stressed in relation to our future evolution and, consequently, to the architecture of the 'real' and 'virtually real' world.

The opening quote is a primitive example of computer poetry based on a simple algorithm (that of

12 In *The Fourth Dimension* (Penguin, 1985, p. 143), Rucker uses the concept of the Minkowski diagram to lead on to the notion that people are 'persistent space-time patterns', and speculates on ideas of life, death and free will in the space-time fabric.

not true that the city is also a collection of specialised homunculi, each conjoined in fluctuating strategies and hierarchies, each with a past that can be traced, both geographically and biologically? Society is about a type of human connectedness. The complexity of the city or a global system is massive: consider the charting of one human module's simple geographical location and interaction with the fabric of the city, let alone that of its infinitely more complex neural (perceptual) counterpart. An easy method of conducting such a charting is the Minkowski diagram,[12] an example of how to record graphically the concept of space-time. Imagine a series of slides of two people moving around a room (in plan, to make the example simpler). A slide is taken every minute, or even every second, and these slides are then arranged in chronological order in a vertical stack, with the early ones at the bottom, the later ones on top. The change in position of each person is mapped from the bottom to the top. This gives the topology of their interaction in space-time (it will produce an intricate pattern of the entwined, contorted tracks that reside in the vertical slide stack). This simple strategy reveals the gorgeous complexity of interaction and knotting that is the result of our constant motion in space-time. Further, imagine the nested nature of these diagrams once not only the body (as a complete unit), but also the limbs, and the articulation of fingers and individual hairs are plotted on to the diagram. Imagine a map of positions in space-time plotted during one day in a single house, street or community. And this would be only a small proportion of a super-Minkowski diagram for a city – or the world – that would also include virtual interactions such as those

digital dreams

producing stanzas by random phrase selection, with rules to negate specific phrase combinations). The computer sampled *The Hiroshima Diary* by Michito Hachiya, *The Mystery of the Elevator* by Paul Goodwin and Lao Tzu's *Tao Te Ching*. The poem is concerned with the fear of technology running out of control. In anti-AI circles this fear is conditioned by a belief in the sacred, infinite complexity of human form and, above all, in human consciousness, and the frighteningly possible fact that in the future we may be able to decode ourselves and create versions of ourselves that will evolve faster than our lethargic, biological time-scale. Of course, the ethical problems are huge; this intervention will serve as a reminder of the urgency for this debate. While it is probably true that Turing's prediction of full AI by the year 2000 will not come to pass, these issues will surely need to be addressed in the early years of the forthcoming millennium.

To return to the specific context of this project, it is proposed that a series of symbolic elements – the Bleeding Heart, the Turing Tower, the Gliders and the Glider-run – are placed within Parker's Piece. The Bleeding Heart is situated at the centre, pierced by the abstract forms of the Turing Tower. The Piece is skinned, its surface removed to reveal the previously invisible veins and arteries of the city – a lesson in the interconnectedness of the biological and mechanical fabric of our lives. This reconciliation will become a matter not of the conjoining of opposites, but of the provision of a new branch in the tree of evolution.

through a modem or telephone, or jumps into full virtual realities such as human dreams and perceptions. Such a continually shifting and knotting tapestry of interaction, although hugely complicated, would no doubt be immensely beautiful. It could well be the 'mind-map' of society.

If some of the crucial parameters for human consciousness are tied up with the notion of connectedness and emergence, could it be said that as the world itself becomes more connected – through cyberspace, information highways and even the simple telephone – it becomes in some sense conscious? Are the phenomena of emergence sewn into the mind-map of society? As this transient infrastructure becomes more and more multimedial, will qualities emerge that start to equate our ideas on society and the city with our ideas on human consciousness? Currently, the informational infrastructure of the world is already sufficiently advanced to herald the genesis of such a sentient supersystem. The first generation of the electronic infrastructure has been well established for some time: the television and the telephone have been familiar household items for many years and we now take for granted the fact that we can see pictures of the Gulf War, Somalia and Bosnia as events unfold, or speak to people anywhere in the world. World-wide mobile telephone networks will further evolve this invisible infrastructure. But it is in the second generation of electronic infrastructure – in the world of computational power and the 'computational dollar' (which will make 'bit' processing available at cheaper and cheaper rates) – that the connectedness of society is set to make a rapid jump. Issues such as the continued compaction of space and the ability of distant action to influence local events, and the fluctuating ethereal nature of physical, mental

The silicon synapses of the future will belong to new species of humanity's parents. We, if successful, will be remaking our elders, our carers and our minders in digital form. Human weakness will be cosseted by machine intelligence even more than it is today. While the forms of the Turing Tower are formally ambiguous, they do carry potent allusions to the continuing technologic shift from the metal armature to the architecture of the protein.

The second group of objects consists of the Gliders and the Glider-runs. The runs are merely a small segment of the infinite Euclidean plane; the Gliders comprise five individual sculptural elements signifying cells with life. The Gliders progress backwards and forwards along the runs, supported and moved by a complex mechanical device. This progress and movement adds another dimension to the proposal, that of time-based 'specialness'. Like other time-based moments that have meaning – such as just before midnight on New Year's Eve or at the putting forward or back of clocks (where time is folded and cut or stretched) – the Gliders return to their original positions, adjacent to the micro-site, at predictable times. The return of the Gliders would be a way of adding a time-based legibility and meaning to the micro-sites. Buildings would be erected on these sites that would have a direct relationship to the 'return of the Gliders'. Throughout their cycle they would be reminders of our dependency on information and our precarious position on the edge of the next evolutionary step. The 'return of the Gliders' on Turing's or Conway's birthday, for example, might trigger AI conferences and such like, or the whole proposal may lie dormant and inert until the Turing Test has been passed, not springing to 'life' until that day.

It is also a distinct possibility that the Glider sculptures will be invested with names, because human beings seem to need to bestow personalities on inert form: perhaps they will be known as 'Sid, Eddie and their friends on an infinite journey' – binary life beyond the realms of death.

13 'I take a pride in probing all your secret moves/My tearless retina takes pictures that prove ...': Judas Priest, 'Electric Eye', 1982, from the album *Screaming for Vengeance*. The issue of surveillance is central to any discovery or invention that can record or predict any human or computational tracks. A full discussion of this area is not within the scope of this book.

and virtual boundaries, will become crucial as these new structures begin to take hold.

If society is seen as a connected entity, a series of parallel processing organisms (each with a smaller, biological, connected, parallel and neural net), it becomes clear that it might be the emergent product of nested, neural, spatial and digital systems. The pandemonium of homunculi posited in the study of consciousness is echoed in the pandemonium of data transfer and social interaction of the city. Maybe the clues to the consciousness conundrum are all around us, in the way that society organises itself.

This seems to push architecture into the realms of connectivity. Architecture must facilitate maximum opportunities for interaction and temporary integration into fluctuating groupings or hierarchic allegiances of homunculi (whether carbon or silicon, neural or societal). These allegiances will form at a variety of scales and many millions (perhaps billions) of times a day; many will form simultaneously as the mind of the city in conjunction with the city of the mind constantly produces the changing scenarios we call reality. What could such an architecture be? One thing is sure; it will in some sense be alive. These are the hurricane years, and they are just starting. But already we are in the steely glare of the tearless retina.[13]

digital dreams

surfing the
surface

It is the intention in this chapter to explore the idea of 'surface', the tactic that nature uses to exclude our perceptions beyond a certain limited bandwidth. As physics and technology grind relentlessly on, this anthropocentric prison's ability to contain the view of our senses is constantly reassessed. How might we appropriate the forces and spaces behind the mask of surface? The world is somewhere behind this mask. The body's prison door is looking more and more fragile.

Whether sitting on a train, walking down a street, travelling in a car or eating a hamburger, we liaise with surfaces. Even as we write we make contact with the surface of the pen, the paper, the table, the floor and the chair. The brain 'jump-cuts' our perception of these forces and sensations as our body constantly reacts to the geography of our environment. At any point in time we are aware of only a few such sensations, but we can tune our perception so that we consciously experience many more. Surfaces are not tied just to gravitational forces and our sense of touch. The background noise of the world is an aural interaction of surfaces, a symphony of impacts. Conversation introduces numerous oral surfaces into this complex weave of perception and demands a specific response. Sight is the momentary recording of the flight of photons – from an object to the surface of the retina. Further, writing is the overlaying of alien molecules on a paper surface. The mark of the pencil is the provision of graphite slag-heaps on the mountainous terrain of virgin paper. There are many metaphysical surfaces available to man's fleeting metaphysical touch, yet he continues to search for more, often with the aid of prosthetic inventions such as binoculars, the telescope, the microscope and the computer. These devices allow him to experience visual surfaces beyond the reach of the unaided eye and, in the case of the computer, to manipulate them. Distance and closeness are essentially the same to man's inquisitive gaze.

We also 'meld' with surfaces, we become them and they us. The simple concept of touch is an impact which leaves its molecular trace on both the toucher and the touched. In the quantum universe there is no void between 'us' and 'it'.

The Forensics of Murderous Manoeuvres

In the realm of the 'macro real', the designer puts together surfaces for the purpose of tactility, functionality, lyricism and enclosure. Site planning is aided by the ability to identify many surfaces and boundaries – some conceptual, some not – both in plan and elevation. This process is currently hugely reductive and has limited results. The elevation is the manifestation of a building that most easily allows us to date chronologically a proposal or context. Its surface is always a pattern of the accumulated cultural baggage that has been handcuffed to its architect's wrist. This weight of culture also determines the viewer's approach to it. The cultures of creator and viewer can be extremely different, perhaps separated by many centuries.

At this scale of 'reality' one of the most crucial issues for architectural consideration is that of how the built intervention interacts with the land surface. Foundations puncture the ground, creating wounds and scars. Archaeology is, in part, the reading of these scars and fragments, much as the topology of the skull provides a fortune-teller's map. The skull map postulates a future; archaeology postulates a past (ground scars often tell of undiscovered clashes of surface). Archaeology reveals past definitions of territory and societal space. Cutting through the silt of time and stripping away recent cul-

It used to be so easy: people simply died, the body was dealt with in some way – normally in a ritual dependent on worldly rank – and then they were remembered or memorialised. But memorialisation is now about to become seriously complex, with two sites of remembrance: the real and the virtual. Each arena has differing environmental criteria and therefore offers differing prospects for ritual or remembering. Real space is heavy, clumsy, inert and slow, while virtual space is fast, light and electroactive. There used to be a single body, without various editions, updates,

tural debris, the archaeologist places together shards of knowledge across space and time. These fragments of previously useful surfaces can be a compass, showing us the way to an understanding of the past. Material can reveal a geographic history, and this can be seen as the beginning of 'surface forensics', a subject which will have great importance for the future of architecture. By studying the ferric ingredients in stone strata, the path of continental drift can be plotted. This is possible because, during the formation of the stone, its preformed silt followed the drift of the continents and the ferric particles aligned themselves in a north–south manner, attracted by the earth's magnetic field. Consequently, the forensics of architectural surface are able to reveal past geography: the large recorded in the small. However, present aspirations tend to influence the interpretation of these fragmentary clues that the earth reveals. So to decode accurately the aspirations of the past we need to cut through the perceptions of the present. Archaeology and architecture must be careful not to see only that which reinforces previous beliefs; they must perceive also the whole gamut of information that the interaction of surfaces can reveal.

Building construction is geared to respond to the forces that act and form surfaces. The silent force in building is the unshieldable force of gravity which constantly pulls surfaces down (forming 'blobs' of glass at the bottom of a pane, for example, as the supercooled liquid battles to hold itself up against never-ending pressure). Much energy and force is consumed in the making of surfaces appropriate for buildings. Materials are sometimes mined from below the earth's landscape plane by a massive induction of energy, and then forced between other alien surfaces to create a building element such

aliases and copies. Now the body is duplicated, recreated, reconfigured, squirted through a variety of invisible pipe-works and smeared across space and time. Decisions will have to be made about what constitutes wet-, soft- and hardware death, much like the guidelines concerning brainstem death in the real world. Any proposal for a system and geography of memorialisation will have to stretch across the boundaries of the real and the unreal so that it can cope with both simple real spaces and complex unreal spaces – and their individual independence and their interaction with each other.

the concrete

as an extrusion or a moulding. Buildings are thus monuments to murderous manoeuvres.

The contrast between different generic surfaces, and consequently between the emotions induced in those who view them, is one of the most powerful aspects of architectural formalism. Contrasting materials – the sleek against the rough cast, the chromed against the rugged – all have a different emotional story to tell. Textural empathy is one of the characteristics of being human, and surfaces are scribed, punctured and extruded to accentuate the emotional perceptions of both user and viewer.

These simple notions of surface, energy and trace will still be appropriate in the future, but their significance will be greatly augmented once our new-found surface hyperaccess becomes common.

At the microscopic and nanoscopic scale, buildings move and fluctuate to accommodate the oscillation of molecules and atoms. The calming influence of relative coldness denies energy and brings the molecules of any material into a more compacted order. Architects must be familiar with many of the techniques used to form buildings; they must know extreme violence and tolerance; they must know the nature of disparate materials and both their macro- and microscopic method of construction. Tolerance is the reason why certain devices – skirtings, architraves, parapets and the like – are used when the architect wants planes to meet and diverge.

The mysterious unseen adds richness to the visible. The surface of the Royal Docks in London is made richer by the knowledge of the accumulated detritus below: the carcasses of Austin 11s, steel beams dropped from cranes – even, perhaps, the bodies of victims of gangland murders.

digital dreams

In our non-virtual 'real' cosmopolitan world, the Christian attitude to memorialisation is obviously not enough. What must be sought is a solution to the question of the complete allegorical gesture. This theoretical solution will have to explore the prima materia of all religious attitudes to memorialisation and produce proposals that are meaningful in themselves yet sufficiently enigmatic for the invocation of any religious preoccupations. Proposals should also consider agnostic and atheistic views. From a study of religious symbolism a mechanism could be evolved that fulfils all these stringent requirements.

Memorials and their gardens are about the 'preciousness of place'. Much precedent exists: burial or cremation has always happened on sacred hills, in sacred churches or on the banks of sacred rivers. We can at once see connections with nature and the seasonal cycles. The proposal illustrated here sites its gardens and structures along the line of the 'meridian' that passes through Greenwich in south London, the line that circles the world and defines Greenwich Mean Time. Actual articulation is left non-specific, but the proviso that all memorial sites should interact with this line is established.

Intuitively, the line/circle implies continuity and infinity. Man takes his place in the ever-

Surfaces pervade our very existence. Our lungs and alimentary tract would not work without the interaction of surfaces. Surface is life. The architect must be a master of surface. Scratching the surface is a noble art.

Implanting the Landscape

As we have seen, the potential spatial qualities of surfaces are as rich and varied as traditional anthropomorphic space, and encompass familiar architectural raw materials such as texture, memory, history, gravity and enclosure. These spaces are ripe for architectural habitation. All that inhibits this occupancy is perception and scale. We cannot see them, get inside them or feel them, but the architecture of the surface is architecture none the less. We are now in the process of developing the necessary tools to allow the colonisation of surfaces, opening them up to our perceptions and ambitions. We need to experience materials not just by smell, colour, texture and the like; we must somehow get closer to them and sense their vitality and inherent contrasts. We must widen the architect's range of possibilities for spatial and material collage.

How might we start to do this? What clues are there around us? This world is not one of simplicity, as our unaided senses conspire to tell us. Once we realise that all around us is in some sense alive, in a constant state of change and exchange, we begin to see the potential of the surface to enhance the drab architectural lexicon. However deeply we penetrate these surfaces, we must not lose our sense of wonder at the notion of 'behindness'. There is always another layer of detail behind: the atom, the neutron, the quark, and perhaps even the superstring. It is at this point that we must transcend the boring certainties of the tradi-

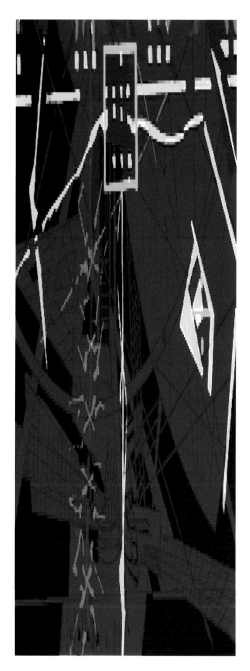

onward flow of time. It has been said that our atomic make-up consists of refugees from the Big Bang and that star-fire therefore exists in all of us. Star-watching teaches us another lesson: that what we see, due to the speed of light and the massive distances involved, is dead, always past, a memory etched in light.[1] This makes us aware that all concepts, even death and reality, are not what they might seem to our limited senses. Memorial gardens are manifestations of the need to celebrate existence. Each memorial must be personal to those still alive and the person who has died.

There is an ease in accepting much of the above; it is not particularly controversial. But once we enter cyberspace, all this will need to be challenged and re-evaluated.

1 'We are all of us doomed to spend our lives watching a movie of our lives – we are always acting on what has just finished happening. It happened at least 1/30 of a second ago. We think we're in the present, but we aren't. The present we know is only a movie of the past, and we will really never be able to control the present through ordinary means. That lag has to be overcome some other way, through some kind of total breakthrough.' Tom Wolfe, *The Electric Kool Aid Acid Test*, Farrer, Straus and Giroux, 1968.

tional architectural canon and hypothesise on a possible future, including notions that are on the edge of science. To perceive the spaces within surface we will have to utilise prosthetic devices, and these may have to be implanted into the brain. The rhetoric surrounding brain implants has already developed to a point of Utopian frenzy. 'The dream involves microchips that you clip into snug contact with your central nervous system for instant fluency in a language you've never heard, for expert systems knowledge of new tech, for a new personality.'[1] This quote is not as immensely speculative as it at first seems. Primitive neural implants are not uncommon and have been around for some time. Some patients have already been subjected to as many as a hundred. At the moment, these implants are usually electrodes which introduce pulses through various locations in the nervous system, creating various effects in the patient. This could be a way for us to augment our sensory skills and experience the elements of the nested surface landscape that is currently denied us. Through virtual reality and other technologies we will be able to manipulate this new landscape, to 'molecularly terraform' it. And it is here that the issue of architectural forensics becomes important. Our experience of molecular space will be greatly informed by the history and genesis of material. Two examples of the same material, for instance, may exhibit disparate spatial criteria, created by differences in the temperature of the casting, in the striations of the die when extrusion takes place, and so on.

The old plaster wall now becomes a labyrinth of tight and cavernous spaces with changing molecular bonding, diverse elemental atoms and an almost infinite range of fascinating

1 *Mondo 2000, A User's Guide to the New Edge*, Thames and Hudson, 1993, p. 36.

There seem to be two distinct possible approaches to a memorialisation in cyberspace. It could be a version of an existing real world memorialisation, adapted to unreal criteria, or, more interestingly, a ritual tailored to the almost magical capabilities of virtual space that have something to do with the issue of hierarchies of duplicated and, perhaps, merged selves.[2] While the real space memorial in this proposal bases itself on the simple geometry of the meridian line, the marker and the articulation of its intervention on the line, the unreal space memorial can have no line, only a type of fractally bifurcating tree structure.[3] Although there is no set alignment, there is potential, ubiquity and fleeting coalitions of

2 'In all probability, Virtual Reality will spawn its own new, formal religions. These may be based on reincarnation, on a form of Christianity, Buddhism or other meditative philosophies, or perhaps on something completely new. But as Virtual Reality is what you want to make it, it could also be a forcing ground of the old Roman and Greek religions, mysticism, or perhaps witchcraft – both white and black. Indeed, a religion based on the concept of Virtual Realities rather than the contents of virtual worlds would be consistent with pagan ideas such as drug-cults or the drug-induced religious diversions such as the Berserkers or the Assassins. And a technology that has miracles as a stock in trade should have no difficulty in providing an appropriate religious selection.' Barrie Sherman and Phil Judkins, *Glimpses of Heaven, Visions of Hell*, Hodder and Stoughton, 1992.

3 'The archaeology of memory reveals a consistent process of visualisation, a mnemonic of places and images which, in Classical antiquity, was an essential element of the rhetorician's art, and involved the imaginary construction and decoration of an architectural space.' Jon Bird, 'The Spectacle of Memory', an essay in *Michael Sandle: Sculpture and Drawings 1957–88*, Whitechapel Art Gallery, 1988.

alignment. What might be the new rituals and geometries of these spaces? The merciless Mercator has no place in this non-place. The 'preciousness of place' is superseded (or super-speeded?). The traditional erasure and denial of mourning are not answers any more. How can we continue to mourn the only partially lost? This partiality will become more and more minimal if the sciences of psychology and computing further entwine. This could lead to the quantifiability of the mind. Cyberspace minds may continue to

rhythms. This terrain might be visually analogous to Gibsonian cyberspace – a geometric order, a virtual reality less virtual than a purely silicon reality. Who knows?

Everything is a product of the 'big bang', including ourselves. We are made of 'star-fire', the same 'stuff' as everything around us. With technology we may be able to inhabit the surfaces of ourselves, the surface landscapes of self – a literal manifestation of 'my body is my temple'. We may be able to flip in and out of these spaces in our perceptions in the same way that we now register individual details of the overall form of objects. We will become a species of scale surfers, surface jockeys. This new landscape may be far more tumultuous than our normal existence: exciting and sometimes frightening. But as we continue our search for sensory experience, this may be no bad thing.

We will be able to encrypt into surfaces, leaving traces of communication for the knowledgeable reader to find. The painter's mark will become a landscape of gaudy emotion; our knowledge will no longer be limited by distance. Another type of transcendence will be achieved simply through closeness. The architect's role will become ever more complex. This can only be good; it is too limiting as it stands.

learn even after the death of the wet intelligence that spawned them and on which they are modelled. Where does death reside, or, indeed, is it fully possible any more?

digital dreams

breaking
the house rules

Gathering the objects into a pile on the dresser, she unscrewed the hairbrush handle and removed a plastic panel from the rear of the brush head … A grey paste oozed from the handle, directed by a reference field within the head. Like slime mould it crept across the table top … The resulting pool of paste and deconstructed objects was contracting into a round convexity. Nano was forming an object within that convexity like an embryo within an egg.

Greg Bear, *Queen of Angels*

The design and architecture of our built environment are stupid. Inertness of thought and practice has been prompted by inertness of product.[1] Currently, designers traverse rocky ground between the fluidity of the concept sketch and the discernible parameters of construction. They are forced into choices from an incredibly limited palette. If for a moment we consider the brick, we can see that many of its perceived advantages are intellectually unsustainable. Its merits, we are told, include its wide range of colours, its human scale, simple jointing methods and ease of procurement – but not its capacity to keep out water. Brick buildings must therefore incorporate many preventative measures, such as damp-proof courses, or even a second wall 75mm behind the exterior wall to stop water penetration and allow space for insulation. A house within a house is a silly idea for the end of the twentieth century.

The hand is gloriously adaptable: holding pens, playing the piano, testing the thinness of paper and picking noses are among the many skills in its infinite repertoire. Which tool the hand becomes is determined by the mental software run on it. But it is a biological machine, a meat tool; it cannot change topological form. What hopes have we in real space and real time of escaping material stupidity? Is it possible to design materials that can change their innate qualities and topologies? The answer, perhaps, lies in nanotechnology.

I would have said that a couple of important benchmarks [towards full nanotechnology] are the first successful design of a protein molecule from scratch – that happened in 1988 – and another one would be the precise placement of atoms by some mechanical means [this has now happened] … At present I would say that the next major milestone that I would expect is the ability to position reactive, organic molecules so they can be used as building blocks to make some stable three-dimensional structure at room temperature.

Eric Drexler, *Mondo 2000*, No. 9

1 This is a comment on both architects and architecture. Firstly, architects are normally trained, generation after generation, by a simple conditioned reflex to please their tutor. The uncareful student inherits his tutor's preoccupations and dogmatic stupidity. This sycophancy has immediate short-term benefits, such as the gaining of serf-like employment and validation by professional bodies, but it is this aspect of architectural education that has left the profession ill equipped to evolve any cultural or scientific validity. Architecture schools are cocooned in their highly specific spaces and illegitimate aspirations, with little or no contact beyond (or even within) a narrow institutional context. Where is the genetic engineer, the mathematician, the quantum physicist, the AI pioneer and the neural biologist in the architectural debate?

Secondly, when architects talk of 'smart' buildings they are usually referring to the same old ones with the addition of a selection of simple prosthetics such as light sensors and small electric motors. Their smartness is invariably the smartness of the trickster.

Imagine a world in which anything is possible: where fabrics pump themselves dry if you get splashed or step in a puddle; where objects can change their form and function many times a day; where anyone can make anything, anywhere, anytime – and where immortality is assured. This is not some fairy-tale world; it could be our near future, a Utopia of superabundance with an infinite supply of infinitely flexible materials.

Vat Nano and Nat Nano

Total dominion over matter has always been within the province of the gods – or at least of a Renaissance alchemic magus or two. The twenty-first century will bring us not spells and incantations, but magical molecular nanotechnology. Until recently, advances in material science have been conditioned by hard engineering and the development of materials that rejoice in their capacity for inertia – low expansion, low contraction, high impermeability and such like – creating specific materials for different jobs. Until now our ability to 'birth' hybrid material, whether organic or inorganic, has been limited by a 'top-down' approach; that is, the process of dissecting the whole into smaller and smaller parts. But recently a 'bottom-up' approach has led to new insights. In the case of consciousness theories, for instance, we are now nearer the creation of hybrid materials and the ability to reconfigure those materials continually. This 'bottom-up' approach has been made possible by our increased dexterity at microscopic levels.

Currently, nanotechnology is more theory than practice but, as time goes by, more and more of its applications are being carried out and understood. Nanotechnology (nano) is the creation of K Eric Drexler[2] and is based on the premise that if we can make self-replicating machines small enough, in the end we will be able to create molecular-sized factories and manipulate matter atom by atom, reconstituting and creating anything. There are two types of nano: wet and dry. 'Dry' refers to the creation of minute, but traditionally mechanical, devices – such as gears, bushes, pumps and levers – from small quantities of atoms to form molecular-sized factories. 'Wet' nanotechnology utilises the replication potential of biological cell division and DNA as its machinery (why bring in more hardware when we have all the wetware we need?). The implications of these types of technology are devastating. Much has been written of the effects of the 'wired' world of cyberspace, but these will pale into insignificance compared to the surreal and magical consequences of nano.

Nanotechnology requires a gestation period, but the gestation itself is exponential: it accelerates as one assembler assembles another, so two becomes four, four becomes eight, and so on. This is the same pattern that bacteria follow and, indeed, nano could achieve a similar speed of reproduction: a generation every twenty minutes. This amazing reproductive potential gives rise to the 'grey goo' problem (see page 99), a fear that should this technology escape control, perhaps by viral infection in its soft- or bioware, it could overrun the earth in a matter of hours – or, as Rudy Rucker puts it: 'The whole planet could end up as a glistening sludge of horny can-openers.'[3]

2 K E Drexler, *Engines of Creation*, Oxford University Press 1992. Drexler's seminal, readable book on the numerous aspects of nanotechnology. His other texts include *Nanosystems: Molecular Machines, Manufacturing and Computation*, Wiley Interscience, 1992, and *Unbounding the Future* (with Peterson and Pergamit), Morrow, 1991.

3 R Rucker, *Mondo 2000*, No. 9, p. 96. This quote is taken from Rucker's introduction to an interview with Eric Drexler entitled 'Vulcan Logic on the Road to Lilliput'.

The gestation period would also require a structure analogous to the womb, a place where the wet raw materials which have been ducted into the womb space – or which were present there before the nano was activated – can be cosseted and held. It is theoretically possible to grow anything in a nano 'vat' or 'matter compiler', as these wombs are called. Drexler's description of the growth of a rocket engine conjures images of foetal development: 'Then the vat's pumps return to life, replacing the milky fluid of unattached assemblers with a clear mixture of organic solvents and dissolved substances – including aluminium compounds, oxygen-rich compounds to serve as assembler fuel. As the fluid clears, the shape of the rocket engine grows visible through the window, looking like a full-scale model sculpted in translucent white plastic. Next a message spreading from the seed directs designated assemblers to release their neighbours and fold their arms. They wash out of the structure in sudden streamers of white, leaving a spongy lattice of attached assemblers, now with room enough to work. The engine shape in the vat grows almost transparent, with a hint of iridescence.'[4]

4 From Drexler's description of growing a rocket engine in *Engines of Creation*, op. cit. pp. 60–63.

This technology will create opportunities for architects and product designers to cater for our fluctuating functional and aesthetic requirements. The products of this technology will be soft, responsive, wet and smart, and they will be grown, grafted and bred.

Nano will also be able to rejuvenate and sustain the longevity of the body's organs and blood highways. How will this fundamental leap in human and technological evolution affect the products on which we have such dependence? Product design creates the prosthetics that expand our normal, lim-

digital dreams

ited human dexterity and enable us to cope with the modern mechanistic world. A simple but radical outcome of nano could be the ability of objects, at the moment of their creation, to reflect what Heidegger called 'worlding'. According to Heidegger, an object is sculpted by prolonged use: for example, a hammer is 'worlded' by use and changes to fit the hand that uses it most frequently. In the same way, a new pair of shoes are uncomfortable until they become 'worlded'. Nano allows objects to be specifically tailored to individual ergonomic criteria at the very beginning of their life. Products would be constructed inside domestic 'matter compilers' or 'vats', growing from a series of molecular raw materials into an infinite array of forms. These machines would only need to be the size of a microwave oven. It would all be just a matter of programming.

Newly constructed objects would immediately take their place within the context of the domestic information ecology. The home would become not only a human habitat but also a habitat for multiple networked intelligences. Once linked together, these individual smart objects will interact to create the meta-intelligence of the home. Such ecologies would live up to the old adage that 'the whole is greater than the sum of the parts'. Consider a pen that never runs out of ink and, when put down for a coffee break, turns the kettle on or, even better, tells the matter compiler to make hot coffee – or, even better still, tells it to make coffee based on a subtle evaluation of your caffeine levels and an understanding of your metabolism and psychology. In time, the material products of matter compilers will not have to comply with even the tyranny of the periodic table. Artificial atoms have already been fleetingly created. Such atoms contain electrons that 'shell' around non-existent nuclei. New and never before imagined materials are

Con 3 The notion of programmed atoms and out-of-control molecules at first seems akin to the plot of a laughable 1950s sci

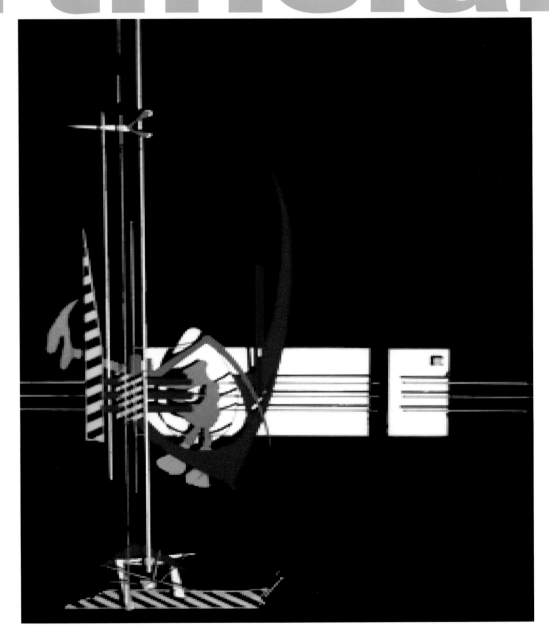

digital dreams

m set in southern Texas, where the architectonic structure and inhabitants are slowly but surely decomposing as they are morphed atom by atom into a malevolent sludge. This would seem a witty and entertaining scenario were it not for the
disconcerting possibility that science has now, theoretically at least, made such a series of eventualities possible. In
nanotechnology this is called the 'grey goo' problem. If atoms can be manipulated singularly, then the integrity of
their software becomes a crucial component of their design. If such software becomes virally infected or bug-ridden,
there is the potential for this most potent of technologies to run riot. The result could be the decomposition of our
material world (including the flesh-and-bone sacks we call our bodies) and the creation of a world of 'grey goo'.
Drexler, the father of nanotechnology, has posited a type of nanotechnological police force (called 'blue goo') that
could be used to enforce the gooey status quo. It would form an active shield, able to isolate and destroy maverick
self-replicating molecules. This technology would have a reproduction rate similar to that of bacteria: one generation

now theoretically possible. Diamond structures will become as cheap as any other structure because they will simply be rearranged carbon atoms. What types of products would benefit from diamonds being a viable material consideration?

Hacking the Husk

Nano will be augmented by genetic algorithms with varying criteria for fitness for survival. It is conceivable that products could be modified using the accumulated experience of many matter compilers and their users. The machines would be smart enough to learn from previous incarnations of products in order to create more effective designs. Both the matter compilers of the future and their products would be equipped with evolutionary intelligence, one informing the other. A shoe, for example, might be able to sense a change in your walk if you put on weight, leading to a propensity to walk unevenly. It could then calculate the extra load on the shoe's left heel, say, and activate nanoreplicators to build up the worn-away layers.

Nano allows buildings and objects to expand and contract and change form – at either a diurnal rate or even continually – in response to a variety of stimuli. Objects large and small will become programmable, dependent on the software in the microscopic 'seed' computer placed in the 'vat' at the initial stage of their reconfiguration. Designs for buildings could self-replicate. A building might well look to its generational ancestors, thus becoming the product of a formal genetic algorithm that determines a search for a 'fitness' of some sort, either aesthetic or functional. Elements of fitness that could be sought might include the optimum length for book shelves; the ideal temperature and thickness of skin; or trends in architectural

every twenty minutes. The icon would be projected on and within areas of 'grey goo' infestation. The 'blue goo' would then force 'nature' back into its previous form or, indeed, could be programmed to turn such crises into constructive opportunities, reconfiguring 'nature' and 'construction' into new biomechanical hybrids. (The distinction between nature and construction becomes erroneous with such a technology.) Further, a fail-safe programming function in all nanotechnological processes could make this icon an automatic byproduct of any nanoprogram failure so that the mutant atomic configuration becomes instantly recognisable as the icon itself. This seems to have the advantage of bringing such problems into the scale of anthropocentric perception. The nightmare of a world 'full of horny can-openers' (as Rudy Rucker has described the 'grey goo' problem) is thus reduced to a vision of iconic outbursts that are quickly and effectively policed.

façades. Obviously, in a nanobuilding the air would always be fresh and the structure thin, light and strong. Honeymoon couples could grow a new home while sunning themselves on a foreign shore, providing a neighbour made sure it did not dry up before they got back.

These examples are but a few of the infinite possibilities of a nanotechnological revolution. It is also clear that the power of the 'aesthetic control police' (consisting of architects, designers and planners) will be eroded as everyone develops the potential to create form. The liberation of every individual's creativity – whether repugnant or beautiful to anyone else – would be fully realisable. Could it be that the future will see an embargo on nano software, much like the provision of the 'v-chip' in televisions? 'Come down to the basement and play cards on my new Barney Rubble card table. What? Yeah, that's real hair. Hell, what's real anymore? Oh yeah, he was a space-shuttle wing last week.' Curiously, the concept of wetness on construction sites is at present anathema to the 'fast-track' system of building; but in the future, wetness could be the major constituent of any successful swift-fabrication method.

Cracking the Code

Other types of seed computers exist in our biological cells. Once we fully understand our genetic codes, gene manipulation will become an everyday occurrence. The body could then be re-engineered to become resilient to disease and old age. Numerous processes could become possible: for example, cryogenic resurrection is made more likely if nanomachines can stitch together the nerves and body tissue of previously frozen bodies. Nano toothpaste, antiperspirant, or even beau-

digital dreams

tiful skin earrings for that special night out, would become a reality. Rudy Rucker, in his fictional *Wetware*,[5] has characters concerned with the acquisition of addictive 'merge' – a type of deconstructive nanotechnology that can be used for a more personal relationship. It would initiate a dissolution of body parts in a vat and cause it to merge with another dissolved body in the vat to achieve a new type of togetherness.

5 R Rucker, *Wetware*, Hodder and Stoughton, 1989. One of Rucker's merge trips is described as follows: 'Stahn slumped back. God this was fast dope. His left arm looked like candle wax, and he was having trouble staying in his chair. He let himself slide down onto the floor and stared up at the ceiling. Oh, this did feel good. His bone joints loosened, and his skeleton sagged beneath the puddle of his flesh…'

One of the most difficult issues that nano raises is that of conscious materials. Buildings and their components could become conscious – alive. Descartes' 'cogito, ergo sum' (translated by Spinoza as 'I am conscious, therefore I exist') then becomes important in relation to the built fabric of our cities. It has recently been said that because some apes have the intelligence of a two-year-old child, apes should be given human rights. In time, when buildings have surpassed this level of intelligence, will they too be given human rights? Would demolition without the building's permission be murder? Perhaps what is needed is a series of laws akin to Asimov's Laws of Robotics, which are:

1 A robot may not injure a human being or, through inaction, allow a human being to come to harm.

2 A robot must obey the orders given to it by human beings except where such orders would conflict with the First Law.

3 A robot must protect its own existence as long as such protection does not conflict with the First or Second Law.

This major philosophical debate, particularly in reference to artificial intelligence, is already taking place within the scientific community – but not in architecture. It is imperative that architects research these avenues because it is in architecture that the philosophical issues of the 'aliveness' of smart materials will first become paramount.

One thing is sure: with the help of nanotechnology, our products are about to become the products of our imagination more than ever before. All that will hinder us is the quality of our imagination, and even that restriction may not exist for much longer. Perhaps we will evolve a machine with an imagination better than a human's. Nanotechnology will not only be 'in your face' – it might be on your face or even sulking because it does not like your taste in music.

the continuing impact of machines[1]

or
A Young Man Intrigued by the Flight of a Non-Euclidean Fly[2]

1 This was also the title of an exhibition featuring surrealist work inspired by machinery, held at the London Gallery, Cork Street, in 1938. This particular endeavour of the surrealists has always interested me; I feel that some sixty years on they would still be amazed and excited at the impact of the machine as technology forces our lifestyles to become more and more surreal.

or
A Young Man Intrigued by the Flight of a Non-Euclidean Fly[2]

2 The subtitle is borrowed from Max Ernst's painting *Young Man Intrigued by the Flight of a Non-Euclidean Fly* (1942 and 1947).

Flies Around Flesh and Flesh Around Flies

Imagine millions, perhaps billions, of micro- and nanoscopic computing machines crawling over your body: in your face, in your eyes and ears, up your nose, in your mouth and down your throat; infesting your lung cavities, swimming in your bloodstream and bathing in your fluids – all battling for survival against each other. Imagine, also, the air full of biomechanical objects borne on air and sound pressures, some almost invisible like pollen, others actually invisible to the naked eye, and yet others the size of insects. This will be part of the environment of the future, where occluded fronts of biomechanical life forms drift or propel themselves within and across bodies and continents. For millions of years natural organisms, particles and spores of many sorts have drifted like so much flotsam and jetsam, looking for a home, a partner or a victim, each recording, learning and reproducing in a dusty maelstrom. The prospect of adding the machine to this flying and floating cauldron of opportunistic life and matter should not be considered contentious. The impact of the machine – from long before the Industrial Revolution up until our cybernetic high-bandwidthed and hyperlinked world of today – is seen by cultural critics as the effects of the evolution of a mechanistic 'other', something more strange and alien than any other human culture could be. The role of humanity – as

Realms and islands were as plates dropped from his pocket.
William Shakespeare, *Anthony and Cleopatra*

Any sufficiently advanced technology is indistinguishable from magic.
Arthur C Clarke's Third Law[3]

3 *Technology 2001: The Future of Computing and Communications*, ed. Derek Leebaert, MIT, 1991.

the agent both of machine coalescence and, currently, of machine evolution – needs to be seen as a passing phase. The era when man is seen as either putty for machines or the selector of fitness, is shortly to end. As a result of our continued research into artificial intelligence and genetics, 'emergence', with its multilevelled and multifaceted hyperstructures, is making us conceive of a very different human ontology. We are forced to come to terms with the notion that the human flesh sac might not be sacrosanct after all, both in terms of advanced consciousness and its ability to act as a barrier against machine invasion and mechanistic desires.

This chapter explores a possible world of the near future. The prediction of the future is fraught with problems, and futurology is strewn with unmet prophecies and fictional futures bifurcating from common pasts. However, the postulation of future events, conditions and parameters is crucial not only to the human situation and artificial intelligence, but also to the subset of human endeavour called architecture. Architects consistently try to predict the near future; they even draw plans of it. In effect, their work has much in common with that of science-fiction writers: they are both authors of virtual futures. It could be argued that architectural design has many distinct and fundamental rules that the science-fiction author does not need to follow: the inherent qualities of materials, methods of jointing and weather tightness, for example. Such problems or opportunities are merely concerned with the local geography of some, but by no means all, terrains of architecture. Here we will navigate an area of the modal domain of architecture that is seldom charted: the aerostat and the biostat,4 small biomechanical machines that exhibit a 'swarm'

4 'Aerostat' is used in Neal Stephenson's *The Diamond Age*, Bantam Spectra, 1995. 'Biostat' is a hybrid word invented by Stephenson to create a distinction, but a generic connection, between in- and out-body machine structures.

digital dreams

phenomenon which emerges from higher-order hyperstructural configurations.5 Our small world will become even smaller; our constructional aspirations will shift from the macro-intervention to the small and minute.

5 Nils A Baas, 'Emergence, Hierarchies and Hyperstructures' in *Artificial Life III*, ed. Christopher G Langton, Addison-Wesley, 1994.

Halo of Flies[6]

The sun is hot, its light bright. A distant buzz is detected on the periphery of your hearing as a small flying bug meanders into view, its black and yellow carapace propelled along its chaotic path by minute wings. But what if this organism hovering in the air is not a wasp or a bee but an aerostat, a small, slightly smart machine structure? None the less, the aerostat, like its biological cousin, will be a product of evolution. And this hybrid creature will be capable of swarming. Such a facility again promotes the notion that 'the whole is greater than the sum of the parts', an adage illustrating a phenomenon known to humanity for millennia. Neal Stephenson, in his science-fiction novel *The Diamond Age*[7] (set on a future earth), describes various security measures taken by enclave factions (particularly the 'New Atlantis Clave') to protect themselves from invasion. These include a 'dog pod grid – a swarm of quasi-independent aerostats'. According to Stephenson such devices are dependent on systems whose miniaturisation and lightness have been brought about by nanotechnology. Each dog pod 'was a mirror surface, aerodynamic teardrop just wide enough, at its widest point, to have contained a ping-pong ball. These pods were programmed to hang in space in a hexagonal pattern, about ten centimetres apart near the ground (close enough to stop a

6 The title of an Alice Cooper song on the *Killer* album; it is said to have inspired Adam Ant's 'Ant Music'. All good swarming stuff.

7 Stephenson, op. cit.

biomechanica

dog but not a cat, hence "dog pods") and spaced wider as they got higher. In this fashion a hemispherical dome was limned around the New Atlantis Clave.'[8] When wind pressure distorted their formation, the pods adjusted their position by using small air turbines; when their batteries became weak they recharged from their neighbour. The system even had 'nurse drones' which could repower 'dog pods' randomly over the grid.

8 Stephenson, op. cit. p. 49.

Another type of flying aerostat structure could well be the Personal Memex. Each Memex would be a 'life file' of its organic partner's life, a record of its owner's life experiences which could be stored for future playback. The Memex could also be accessed as a personal library – the ultimate photographic memory. The concept of the biography will become extinct as the autobiography becomes so much more believable, immediate and pure – providing the information is highly encrypted and thus difficult to hack.

As well as 'dog pods' Stephenson also describes 'immunocules': 'It was foggy in the Leased Territories, because all of the immunocules in the air served as nuclei for the condensation of water vapour. If you stared carefully into the fog and focused on a point inches in front of your nose, you could see it sparkling, like so many microscopic searchlights, as the immunocules swept space with lidar beams. Lidar was like radar except that it used the smaller wavelengths that happened to be visible to the human eye. The sparkling of tiny lights was the evidence of microscopic dreadnoughts hunting each other implacably through the fog, like U-boats and destroyers in the black water of the North Atlantic.'[9] These battles – where factions of air-borne immunocules battle against one another, disabling each other

9 Stephenson, op. cit. p. 52.

digital dreams

anitestructur

hyperstructure

and falling to earth – are wittily termed 'Toner Wars' because they create a layer of dust on other objects, like photocopier toner gone wild.

Lilliputian machines such as these are not constrained to the outside of the subject organism; they will also be able to access the subject itself. This biological penetration will be fundamentally symbiotic; however, various biomechanical organisms – parasitic or pathogenic (pathocules) – will undoubtedly be a downside of such technology. The widespread synthesis of the biological and the mechanical will become neither remarkable nor even recognisable, and this trend can already be seen in certain medical procedures.

Hollow Core Humanity

The advent of the human brain on the stage of the universe makes nature obsolete.
David Porush's Law[10]

The body, whether human or non-human, will become host to an ever-increasing variety of biomec prosthetic immunocules and pathocules, who will be joined, perhaps, by nanophages and macrophages as well as by numerous other hybrid nouns used to describe the body's new-found biomec populations. The lack of nanotech structures in a body may well be termed nanaemia. The consciousness corpuscle of the body will have been reinforced and re-engineered to remove many of the mistakes of wet historical evolution; in the process it will have been supertuned to increase both the speed of information-processing and its durability. The performance artist Stelarc has recognised that the flesh cage could potentially be the downfall of wet consciousness: 'The Hollow Body would be a better host for technological components.'[11] Ultimately,

10 Porush's Law was quoted in his presentation abstract for the 'Virtual Futures Conference' at the University of Warwick, England, 26–28 May, 1995.

11 Stelarc, 'Towards the Post-Human', in *Architectural Design*, Profile No. 118, Architects in Cyberspace, eds. Neil Spiller and Martin Pearce, November/December 1995.

digital dreams

nanite

such life- and information-enhancing technology could also be used as a fashion accessory. As our visual, aural and tactile perceptions are raised to a higher bandwidth, fashion and fluctuations in the criteria for beauty will invade other wavelengths. Long-chain nanite structures might be programmed to grow into complex, intricate patterns within the dermis, or be decorously draped around the colon to create x-ray jewellery. x-ray evaluation of the body may well become more widespread and, perhaps, be used also for aesthetic enjoyment.

The Magic of Mini, Micro and Molecular Machines
Individually programmed robots, capable of acting out various scales of tasks, have been difficult enough for our recent forebears to imagine. Yet the usefulness of an individual machine is limited and so is only a small component of the future-machine ecology. The swarming or flocking of machine colonies will become the norm. The dynamics of such communities will be learnt from the biological phenomena of emergence. These are the qualities shared by groups of things – for example, ants, bees, locusts and many other creatures and structures (not necessarily biological) – but which are not present in the individual unit. Geese flying in formation is an example of emergent behaviour. A higher-order system or structure emerges through the complex, non-linear dynamic of a group of 'primitive' structures or systems. Emergence has been intimately connected with concepts of evolution. The magic of emergence is that it cannot be predicted. A dynamic system must be allowed to run and run until the phenomenon manifests itself. The systems or structures that are prone to emergent criteria are called hyperstructures. Examples of these are higher-order organisms and 'general technological constructions designed in a modular

digital dreams

12 Baas, op. cit. p. 526.

or levelwise way and metatype constructions in system theory'.[12] Hyperstructures consist of primitives – in this case a series of minute machines – and from their interaction a series of second-, third- or n-order structures and systems emerges. These phenomena have been shown to evolve in experiments in artificial life (A-Life)[13] and are suspected by some to be at the root of consciousness. Could a break in hyperstructural space create artificial or biocell cancer?

13 Baas, op. cit. p. 527.

Sex[in(g)] the Machine

Higher-order organisms have various methods of reproduction. Each method scrambles the parents' genome. Such a shuffling of the pack of genes is critical to the continuing evolutionary trajectory of the species. Darwinian evolution seems on the surface to be one-way, since it takes little or no advantage of any parental occupation-specific characteristics. The Olympic swimmer's muscular torso has to be remade in any second-generation offspring wishing to pursue the same sport. It is not genetically coded into the family genome; if it were, this would be an example of Lamarckian evolution. Such a mechanism used as an evolutionary aid would be of great advantage: an organism could reprogramme its genes as it developed and adapted itself within its hyperstructural context, both internal and external to the body. The biostats and aerostats would evolve Lamarckianly; the evolutionary process would cease to be prone to such a ponderous pace.[14]

14 Kevin Kelly, *Out of Control: The New Biology of Machines*, Fourth Estate, London, 1994, p. 305.

The biological machines of the future would be able to create this genetic feedback loop. Their evolutionary responsiveness would far outstrip our unaugmented stasis. Most of these cultures of fast-

digital dreams

toner

breeding reactive machines will exist in a symbiotic relationship with us, breeding for our mutual benefit. The introduction of sex into the machine liberates us from what Manuel de Landa calls our status as 'insects pollinating machines that do not have their own reproductive organs right now'.[15] This liberation comes coupled with a loss of human control over the machine – the price of emergent machine ecologies. With such an advance the study of many disparate disciplines will become further coalesced to create new hybrid hyperspecialities and, perhaps, even a new epistemology. Anthropology, for example, would branch into nanthropology (the study of nanobiostats) and vanthropology (the study of the virtual ants that are used in the research of artificial life), as well as various other new categories of human classification and evaluation.

15 Manuel de Landa interviewed in 'Manuel de Landa Observed' by Erik Davis in *Mondo 2000*, No. 8, Fun City MegaMedia, 1992, p. 48.

The Hypertrophy of the Machine

Our globe is becoming an arena for a silent liquidity of information movement, as mechanistic colonies drift or are propelled in the bloodstream or weather systems, or communicate through rhizomatic optical fibres and satellite networks. It is a well-known fact that the insect biomass far outweighs that of the mammal. And in years to come it seems likely that machine mass will rival or exceed insect mass, but by then the distinction may have become so blurred and useless that to think in such a way would be folly.

It could be construed as ironic that the domination of the machine will have come about as a result of its reduction in scale – to the point where it is no longer immediately recognised as a machine. Less is more. The next time the alarm clock buzzes, think on!

digital dreams

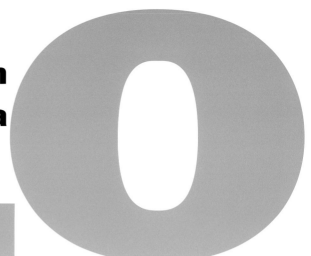

hotdesking in
nanotopia

In his book *Being Digital*,[1] Nicholas Negroponte extols the virtues of the inherent flexibility and speed of transmission of bits as opposed to atoms. The advantages of the virtual over the substantial may be short lived. One day, could atoms, too, be manipulated and programmed, thus gaining the advantages of 'bittyness'? Atoms could combine their ability to make real with the transmutability of information bits. Such an eventuality would allow the bit a ubiquitousness now unavailable outside the cathode-ray conduit or the liquid-crystal display. The bit's escape could be aided and abetted by a branch of engineering that is rapidly gaining converts in the scientific community: nanotechnology. The impact of this idea could shrink further the mechanistic armature to unbelievable minuteness, causing the machine, to all intents and purposes, to disappear. While cyberspatial evolution has been hyped ever onward, nanotechnology, its chronological twin, has been ignored in most discourses on futurology.

1 N Negroponte, *Being Digital*, Hodder and Stoughton, 1995.

In the same way that one does not normally write about cyberspace without crediting the creator of the word, William Gibson, one cannot evoke nanotechnology without mentioning its main advocate and designer, K Eric Drexler. Since the late 1970s Drexler has postulated theories and designed a series of devices that operate at the scale of the nanometer: the scale of molecules.[2] Nanotechology uses these scaled-down versions of solenoids, pipes and pumps to create microscopic 'factories' of assemblers and disassemblers. These diminutive installations have the ability to reconfigure all matter, atom by atom, creating a conceptual Utopia of superabundance – and thus an architecture of cheap and infinitely malleable materials.

2 K E Drexler, *Engines of Creation*.

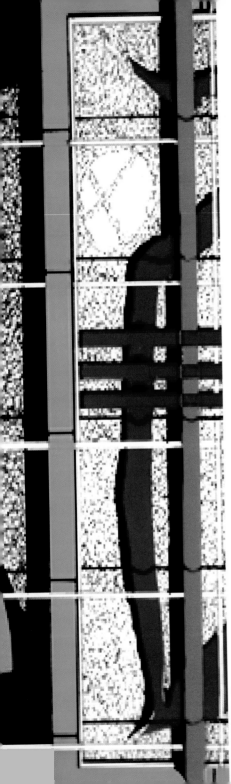

The Nanolithic Age

We are on the cusp of what I shall call the Monolithic and the Nanolithic Age: at the beginning of Nanotime. We have at last sensed that the tyranny of formal inertia is coming to an end. Some of our crucial nanotools, however, are still only at the dream stage, and operating at this scale is like a surgeon working in boxing gloves. But as every day goes by, our microscopic tool shed is becoming stocked with more and more implements that will move us, theoretically, towards total molecular dexterity in the battle to make nature ours. We have started on a track that will ultimately encourage the husbandry of all atomic arrangements and their material results.

Technology has become both magician and assistant: the agent of disappearance and the subject of that disappearance. The machine becomes a 'prompt' at the side of the stage's molecular song-and-dance routine. I sense that there will be further nanological eras or ages, much like the geological stages that aid our classification of the geomorphic layers of landscape. Similarly, the Nanological Ages will be used to chart the evolution of the mobility and erosion of certain forms. If we are now at the beginning of the Nanolithic Age, one supposes that the subsequent age will be classified as the Plasticine Age, where materials are gently morphed or transformed by only one quality, such as flexibility, colour or tarnish. And the age after that might well be the Panacea Age, characterised by the widespread use of nanotechnology as an internalised prosthetic. The Panacea Age would provide cures for all ills, including old age. Intelligent nanomachines would patrol the bloodstream, removing malignant or benign detritus that the body's white blood cells have been unable to deal

digital dreams

with. The medical applications of the nanotechnological machine, or nanites as they are starting to be called, are almost infinite.

Another stage might be the Protoplasmic Age, an era when the body's sensibility and information-processing abilities are so amplified that the whole material world becomes a series of nested arenas of computability: we would then see the evolution of the nanocyborg. This is where cyberspace becomes truly biological. When virtual reality becomes real, the liberation of the bit is complete. The Marvel of nanotechnology will be able to produce Spidey and the Hulk for real; the elasticity of the body, to name but one comic-book attribute, will be assured.

From the Bottom Up

Nanotechnology is a 'bottom-up' science, starting from the interaction of the component parts of a system and, through them, to the generation of a more complex set-up. 'Top-down' technologies are also pushing at the barriers of miniaturisation; small machines such as colon-crawlers and arterial plague-scrapers are already in prototype form. Concurrent with these diminutive machine experimentations is the use of biotech gene splicing – for example, on *E. coli* bacteria to force them to produce human insulin. (*E. coli* is the bacterium commonly responsible for the infection cystitis.) Coincidentally, the same bacteria have been viewed by scientists as a lesson in how Drexler's nanites might either propel themselves or pump fluids. This theory is based on the bacteria's flagella, a hair-like propulsion system which can generate 6000 revolutions per minute at body temperature, and up to a maximum of 38,000 revolutions per minute at higher temperatures,

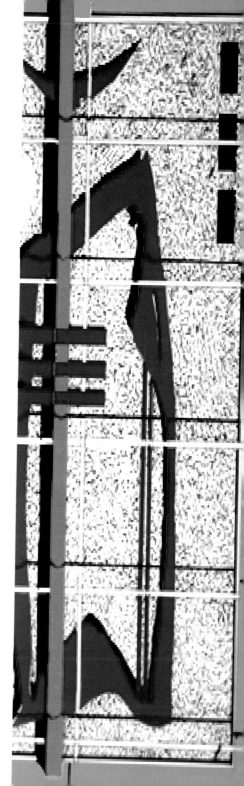

before burn-out occurs. With the technology already provided by nature – and its subsequent supercharging by humanity – biological computers become a distinct possibility. In a few years – and I do mean a few – bacteria will become fully computable. Some believe that full synthesis between nanotechnology and the human body will have occurred by 2014. If such computational power is realised, the bacteria on a typical work surface could provide more computing power than currently exists in all the world. If every surface becomes not only computational but also, through nanotechnology, a surface of formal reconfiguration, then the hermetic vessel of alchemy (the alembic, the site where materials are transformed) assumes the depth of the bionano mono-layer – one bacterium thick, or perhaps even less. The womb of nature would thus be set in the arena of surface tension. Crazy? Maybe; but the successful printing of one-molecule-thick mono-layers for circuits has already been achieved. Any surface will have the potential to be the demiurge's clay, or the anvil of the gods.

Desktop Theatres

In her seminal book *The Art of Memory*,[3] Frances Yates describes the evolution of various memory systems, from the classical mnemonic recorded by Cicero and others, through the memory theatres of Robert Fludd, to the occult memory wheels of the Renaissance magi Giordano Bruno and Ramón Lull. The mnemonic device of the memory theatre depends on the formulation and inhabitation of mental architectural places (*loci*), each specifically honed with images (*imagines*). The consequent interrelationships between the *imagines* and the

3 F Yates, *The Art of Memory*, Routledge and Kegan Paul, 1966.

digital dreams

loci provide a strategy for the 'mind's eye' to 'see' and store many complex concepts. Such systems were used to memorise speeches, songs and religious cosmology. Yates was prophetic enough to recognise similarities between these mental structures, particularly between Bruno's and the 'mind' machines of the time when she was writing (the mid 1960s). This strand of thought was picked up at MIT's Media Lab, where the relationship between image and location was used as a way to represent and store information on a computer-controlled screen. The spatial data management system (SDMS) that was subsequently developed included an electronic picture window and a 'wired' Eames chair. Negroponte describes it as follows: 'The user could zoom and pan freely in order to navigate through a fictitious two-dimensional landscape called Dataland. The user could visit personnel files, correspondence, electronic books, satellite maps and a whole variety of new data types …'.4 The SDMS was populated with a series of icons, and the relationship 4 Negroponte, op. cit. p. 110. between the *imagine* and the *locus* was established as an advanced user interface. The concept then evolved into the now-familiar Apple desktop. With the aid of folders, files, archives and menus the user of the desktop can construct complex interactions of information. This system of connections has a specific yet flexible architecture. The desktop also provides a danger-spot (albeit covered with a detachable safety net), a single area of destructive power in this landscape of constructive opportunity – the trash can. The 'can' is a recycler of memory, the gaping mouth of the void, hungry for malformed or ancient bits and bytes. The current Apple desktop is an ascalar topology – a hi-tech palace of the mind situated in fields among fields.

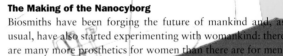

The Making of the Nanocyborg

Biosmiths have been forging the future of mankind and, as usual, have also started experimenting with womankind: there are many more prosthetics for women than there are for men. Meanwhile, as man remakes woman in the magazine image, the much-trumpeted cyborg is about to be nanoed. As Charles Ostman has said, in a recent interview with *Mondo 2000*, nano offers exciting 'modification(s) made directly to the human body'. He cites the example of a German electronics manufacturer who has invented 'a seminal duct implant designed to electrocute sperm before they leave the body'. Tumours will be dismantled by smart nanites, and even by molecular-scaled supercomputers inserted into the existing neural net, augmenting the brain's already awesome capabilities. Such neural enhancement, when possible, will probably create a two-tiered civilisation: those with and those without the advantage of neural upgrading. This is just one of the major problems among the many ethical and philosophical issues surrounding such technology. The prospect of us being 'all Cray-z now' seems remote in the context of the prevailing capitalist system. But even so, nanotechnology's effect on world capitalism remains to be quantified; in theory it could lead to its demise. One thing is sure: this technology opens up a world of surreal or hyperreal aesthetic experience. Could it conceivably allow the nanocyborg to grasp objects, ornaments or icons (they are all the same in nanotopia) and read information directly through its hands and fingertips? In the face of nanotechnology, unassisted evolution is dead: it is too slow and makes too many mistakes. The psychologists' much-debated bipolar discussion in relation to human physical and social development is about to go tripartite, as behaviour and

hotdesking in nanotopia

digital dreams

hotdesking in nanotopia

genetic coding (nature and nurture) are joined by the machine code influence.

Anvil of the Gods

What of the future, where the virtual becomes really real, oscillating in and out of solidness, and where every surface is a neural network with the potential to create the Garden of Eden or Babylon, at any scale, and at the flick of millions of nanoscopic switches? If we achieve total control of nature, nature will cease to exist – a casualty in the collision between nature and technology at speed. The landscape would become purely artificial and artefactual, with its binary-coded fictional narrative told millions of times a second. The nano object will have to take its place in an environment where objects contain various scales of information: symbolic, functional, memorial, and such like. So the design and construction of objects and memory structures in the Real Reality Engine – as opposed to the Virtual Reality Engine – will be fundamentally different (the latter depending on atomless bits, the former on bits of atoms). The 'Anvil of the Gods' project seeks to chart the concepts that will help us quantify some of the opportunities of these impending technologies. The 'Anvil of the Gods' is the desktop (a nanodesktop) of the near future. Such devices are intrinsically difficult to describe because any description is always dependent on lexical and typological constructs, some of which are likely to disappear as a consequence of this technology – but we must try. Such a nanotechnological device might not always choose to exist at desktop scale: it could be palm-sized or even smaller, or it could suddenly increase in scale, or exist simultaneously at a variety of scales. A nanodesktop could be like the board for a game of multidimensional complexity populated by a mixture of the mundane, the weird and the downright crazy. What would such a thing do? What would it be like?

Firstly, it is important to introduce a formal scenario. This can be done by creating three nano icons, each an icon in the traditional computing sense. Each carries 'within' it a narrative concerning issues that may emerge as important in the future. These icons act as the imagines, and a table on which they are situated acts as the locus. The table-top and its supporting structure become an active field of multidimensional proactivity, creating formal interventions which can store information. Nanotechnology at this level is perhaps understood as a series of currents or turbulences of formal potential between two fields – the desk and the air.

It's a Real Pea-Souper, No Mistake

How can the air around a nano object be considered the macro field of interaction? With minor engineering and programming, air can be made into transparent and receptive Utility Fog. The conceptual framework for such a fog was laid down, by Josh Hall,[5] as something which could prevent whiplash in car accidents. Essentially, the dream consists of the notion that nano-doctored air will be able, in a split second, to solidify and cushion us from a dangerous impact. Once this approach is achieved, and it seems that there are no particular insurmountable physical problems, it will be possible to conjure objects or fluids from thin air. We will then have arrived at a final nano age – the Magicio-kinetic Age – when the Magician returns and technology and magic meet again; when telekinesis and all manner of psycho-kinetic arts will be avail-

5 E Regis, *Nano – Remaking the World Atom by Atom*, Transworld Publishers, 1995. Josh Hall's Utility Fog is described on p. 218.

able to all-comers. So this infinitely thick but infinitely thin fog will be the large desktop, a global ether from which existence is conjured. It will be possible to splice together all ornaments, icons or atomic substance – call them what you will – to form hybrids, or they may even be susceptible to the constant nibbling of the nano ether. As one 'launches' icons onto other icons, allowing one to consumme another, nano objects – and, let's face it, all objects – will become nano-morphable; that is, able to create various information hierarchies.

What's in Store? From the Mundane to the Divine

At the scale of the normal family house, the desktop situated in the makeshift study in the spare room – or just the makeshift spare room (we don't all study, you know) – might have a mundane yet highly liberating use. It could have the ability to deconstruct objects and act as a storage unit: something that shreds objects but is capable of reassembling them when necessary, thus solving the 'real' world problem of domestic storage space. Interestingly, such a technology might also solve the 'book/screen' problem. This concerns the known fact that people prefer to curl up in bed with a book rather than a plastic laptop display and assorted manipulation devices such as mice, trackballs or even finger-tickling erogenous pad zones. The book could now become fully digital, reconfiguring from thin air into the weighty leather-bound tome or dog-eared paperback to which we have all become accustomed. Our own books could be digital yet coffee stained (staining would be an obvious menu option, like the removal of hairs or dust caught in the spine), or otherwise personalised in a variety of ways. The library would become the black-hole trash can where molecules are torn asunder and

digital dreams

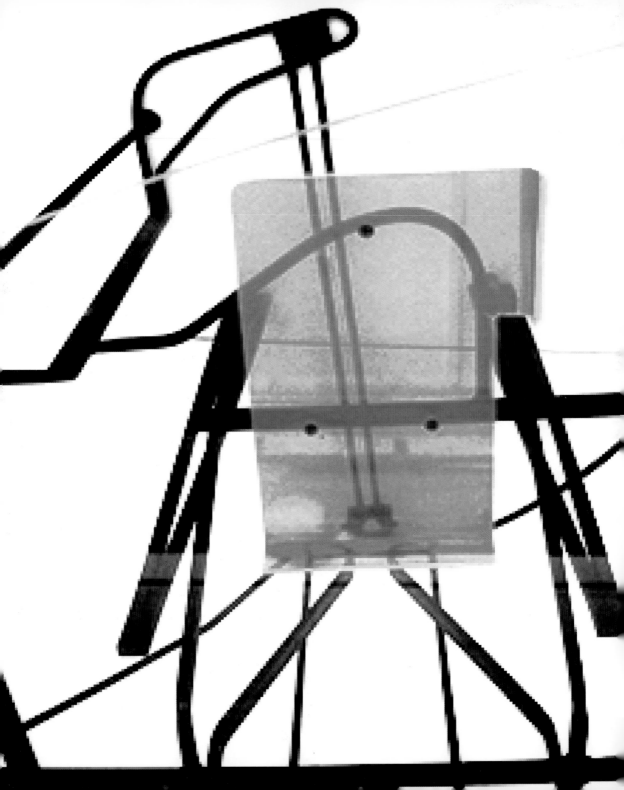

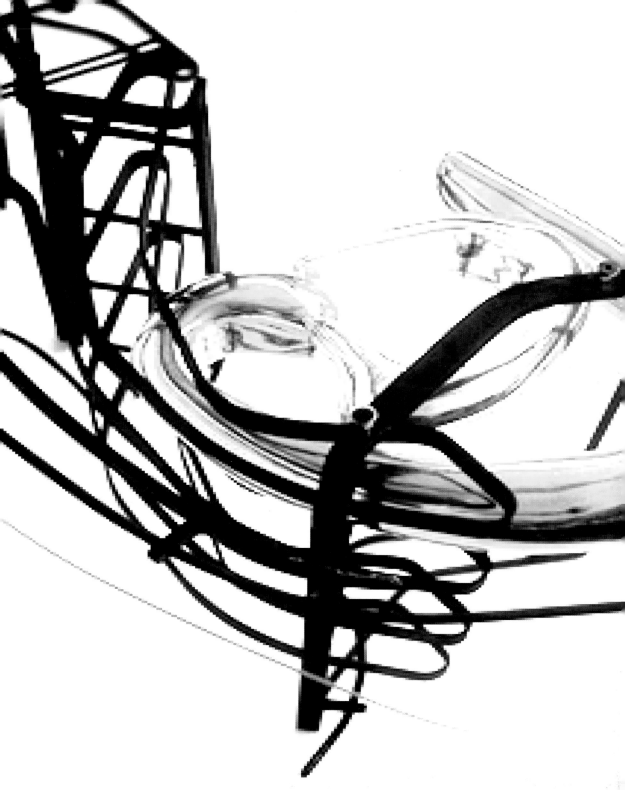

thrown into an anti-matter (or anti-anthropomorphic-matter) universe to await the demiurge's summons of materiality.

Nano-Deskworld™ is also Nano-Dreamworld™, a world where the Burroughsian jump-cut happens not just in text or in theories about the art of the real, but in the creation of actual synaesthetic formal articulations that will for the most part be useless. Yet some will provoke profound and revealing ideas and hybrids of ideas that were previously unimaginable. The nanodesktop's multidimensional screen saver, a type of 'hyper-nirvana',[6] will enable it to push machine thought into matter, allowing the desktop to dream of not only electric sheep but also edible duvets (patterned with the cuttlefish's pulsating colour-morphing skin?) which, once eaten, taste of cardboard with a slight hint of Parmesan. But this is a small-scale idea; what of the divine and cosmic? Baudrillard might well rejoice: it seems that this technology is about to become one of the final names of God that, once uttered or recorded, will bring about the disappearance of the universe.[7]

6 Nirvana™ is a screen saver which appears in a different form every time. It is characterised by psychedelic and constantly mutating screen patterns. Acid for computers.

7 J Baudrillard, 'The Perfect Crime', extract from a lecture at the ICA, London, transcribed in *Wired*, 1.02: 'This is the same as Arthur C. Clarke's fable about the names of God. In that, the monks of Tibet devote themselves to fastidiously transcribing the 99 billion names of God, after which, they believe the world will be accomplished and the end will come. Exhausted by this everlasting spelling of the names of God, they call in some IBM types who install a computer to do the job. A perfect allegory of the achievement of the world in real time by the operation of the virtual. As the technicians of IBM leave the site, they see the stars in the skies fading and vanishing one by one.'

The Weathering of Form

If such desks are but micro turbulences in a chaotic, turbulent, macro Utility Fog (the Big Desktop in the Sky), we could then create a visionary geography, a hybrid of cybergraphy and nanography. The world would become a series of geographical icons, a dreaming landscape or a landscape of memory. And it is here that our physics of space and matter bring us full circle to more arcane religious views of the world

digital dreams

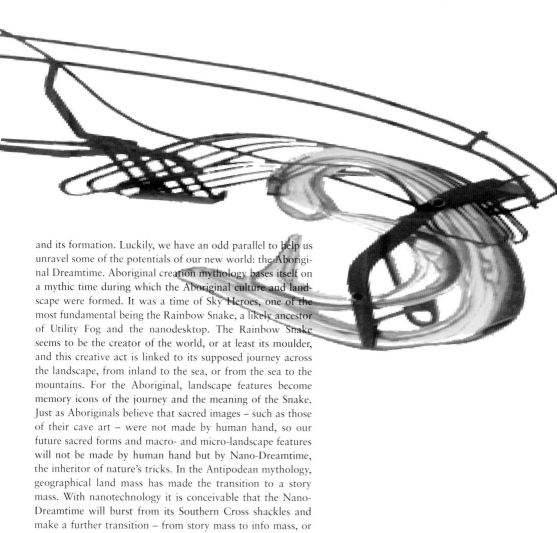

and its formation. Luckily, we have an odd parallel to help us
unravel some of the potentials of our new world: the Aboriginal Dreamtime. Aboriginal creation mythology bases itself on
a mythic time during which the Aboriginal culture and landscape were formed. It was a time of Sky Heroes, one of the
most fundamental being the Rainbow Snake, a likely ancestor
of Utility Fog and the nanodesktop. The Rainbow Snake
seems to be the creator of the world, or at least its moulder,
and this creative act is linked to its supposed journey across
the landscape, from inland to the sea, or from the sea to the
mountains. For the Aboriginal, landscape features become
memory icons of the journey and the meaning of the Snake.
Just as Aboriginals believe that sacred images – such as those
of their cave art – were not made by human hand, so our
future sacred forms and macro- and micro-landscape features
will not be made by human hand but by Nano-Dreamtime,
the inheritor of nature's tricks. In the Antipodean mythology,
geographical land mass has made the transition to a story
mass. With nanotechnology it is conceivable that the Nano-
Dreamtime will burst from its Southern Cross shackles and
make a further transition – from story mass to info mass, or
perhaps even info weather, a dream theatre of
global proportions. The Aboriginals 'recognise
that the natural object is capable of being imbued
with supernatural power'.[8] This supernatural
power concerns itself with the synthesis of the natural object and its symbolic shadow or double. For Aboriginals, every natural thing has totemic identity; this duality links
the viewer into the Aboriginal grand narrative and provides
navigational signposts, both metaphoric and physical. It is
clear that in the future it will be harder and harder to separate

8 J G Cowan, *The
Elements of the
Aborigine Tradition,*
Element Books, 1992.

the augmented human form (or nanocyborg) from its Utility Ether and, further, that the concept of weather will have to be reassessed in the light of Nano-Deskworld and Nano-Dream-time. Strange weather indeed. Will the architect become a formal meteorologist?

digital dreams

leaving nadir

Cyborgian Mutation and Architecture

... mindbody meatbody deathbody stinking sagging shitting fetus bursting organs hanging buried alive in a coffin of blood oh god not me don't let it be me got to get out of this bucket of tripe it's sucking me down throwing me up take it away this pulsing writhing spurting spinning body-go-round, BODY ...1

1 D Skals, 'Antibodies', in *Isaac Asimov Presents*, ed. Gardiner Dozois, New York, 1988.

The Changing Carcass

The architectural subject is changing (with 'subject' meaning both the body and the practice). Traditional notions of architectural enclosure are unable to respond to the growing range and virtuosity of the body, and this is an escalating problem. Architectural theory has been slow, if not frighteningly inert, in understanding and facilitating the metamorphosis of its own subject, both spatially and biologically. Our spacescape and our bodies are two interacting fields: as the spacescape is transcribed by the constantly mutating body, it changes accordingly. The observer changes the spacescape simply by the act of operating within these fields. Much has been written in post-modern literature of the concept of the cyborg: the machine-and-flesh hybrid that contemporary technology has made, and continues to make, of the body. The evolving symbiotic relationship between the cyborg and the spacescape is crucial to the development of a pre-industrial discipline such as architecture. We need to explore and record the various states of the spatially transcribing biomechanical structure that we refer to as the body, and to postulate on its impact on the architectural spacescape.

There are many flesh chauvinists, and while one does not want to call into question the undeniable pleasures of inhabiting the body, these flesh Luddites seem unwilling to recognise that the integrity of the body is in shreds – torn, ripped and cut by technologies that have steadily multiplied in effect and number throughout the twentieth century. The body is imploding and exploding all at once – and so, therefore, must architecture. However, the transition from states of implosion and explosion, and vice versa, is smooth and lacks a jolted boundary. Perception now swings both ways: with medical

technology we look inwards; with media technology, out-
wards. It is conceivable that as the ontological distinctions
between 'mechanical' and 'biological' disappear, so too will
concepts of distance.

Grow Your Own

The body, so precious and intimate to us, is an area of human
culture fraught with hysterical gibberish about the sanctity of
the flesh cage. It may be wise, therefore, to take a couple of
opinions from the medical profession, which is relatively
untainted by the ongoing distrust of professional structures
that is found in other disciplines such as architecture and the
law. The mystical power of medical technology and methodol-
ogy offers us a conceptual escape route that responds to a
yearning for longevity – some respite or insurance against the
death taboo.

    The first medical experts we will consult are Robert
Langer and Joseph P Vacanti, who assure us that in the near
future the growing of artificial organs and limbs will be of as
little medical consequence as the giving of blood is now. In
their essay 'Artificial Organs',[2] they lead us through
the techniques that will be employed in the creation
of an artificial hand and arm which could be grown
around biodegradable plastic. 'The structure of each
system – muscle, bone, blood vessels, skin and so on
– would be duplicated in biodegradable plastic.
These "scaffolds" would then be seeded with cells of relevant
tissues. The cells divide and the plastic degrades, finally only
coherent tissue remains. A mechanical pump would provide
nutrients and remove wastes until the arm, which would take
roughly six weeks to grow, can be attached to the body. Most

2 R Langer and J P Vacanti,
'Artificial Organs', in *Scientific
American* – Key Technologies
of the 21st Century,
September 1995.

                                                  digital dreams

of this technology is already in place. The remaining hurdle is the regeneration of nerve tissue.'

Human skin grown on polymer substrates has already been used to help patients with severe burns or skin complaints such as ulcers. In the same article Langer and Vacanti also promote the use of microchips, or 'visionchips', to cure certain blinding diseases that attack the retinal surface but leave the nervous infrastructure of the eye intact. They also see artificial wombs as near-future possibilities. The ability to create flesh and organs outside the evolutionary equipped womb could well lead to a flesh fecundity – the prolific growing and use of artificial flesh.

Another medical physician, Dr Rachel Armstrong, in her essay 'Post-human Evolution',[3] reminds us that 'Genes operate randomly by the process of Natural Selection and produce mutations through methods over which we have very little control. With current advances in biotechnology and intelligent systems, the ability for humans to be instrumental in directing their own evolutionary strategies is now possible. We are able to make designer mutants, beings who could not exist without considerable intervention.' Armstrong is a medical consultant to performance artist Orlan, of whom we will hear more later.

3 Dr R Armstrong, 'Post-human Evolution' in *Artifice*, Bartlett School of Architecture, University College London, 1995.

Visceral Escapology

Let us for the moment leave the subject of Matter and the New Flesh and consider the body's shadow: the cyberspatial cyborg, which, in its many split and shared forms, can be sustained only in virtual worlds. The body and its cyberspatial agents are but different manifestations and versions of the

from genesis

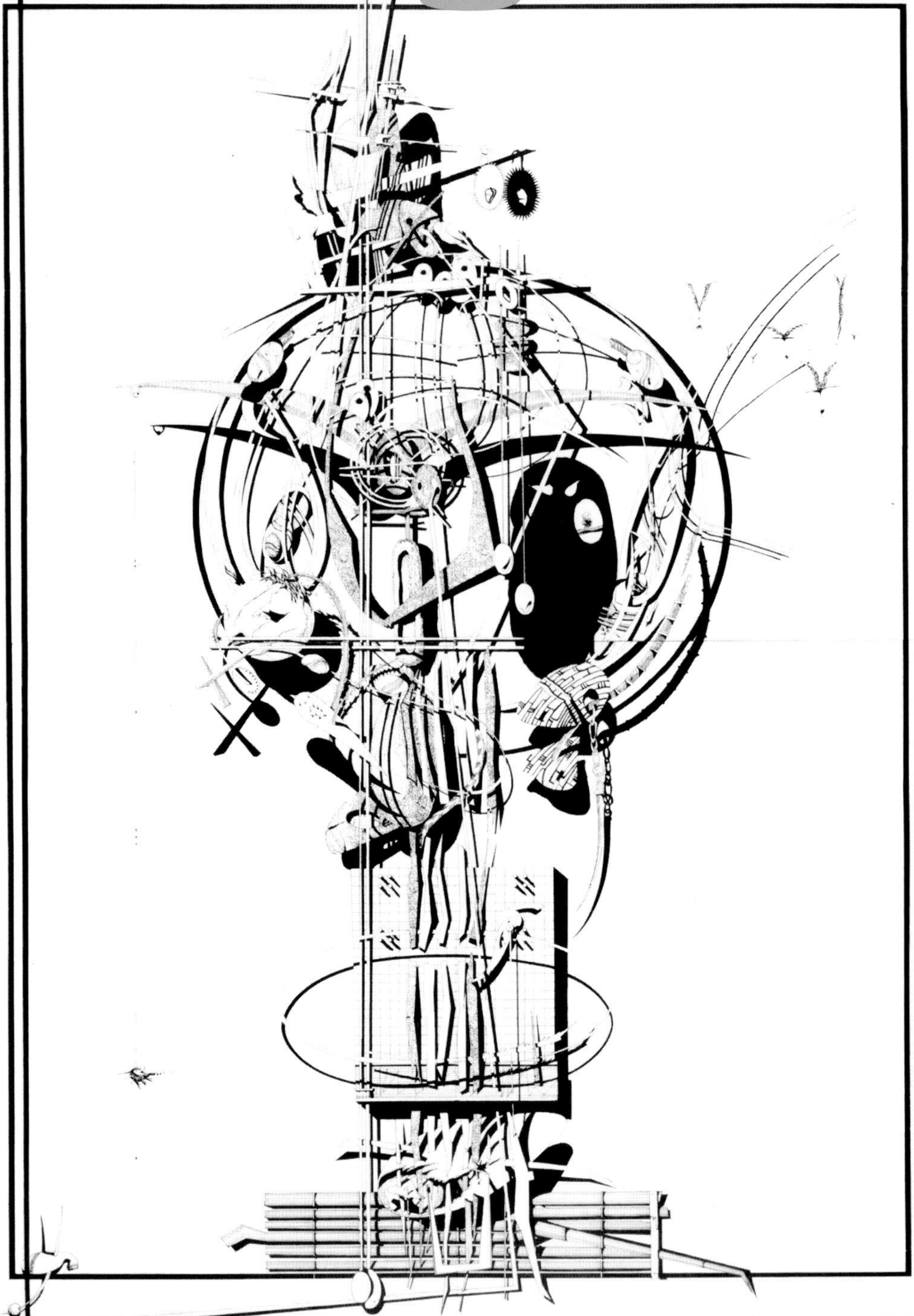

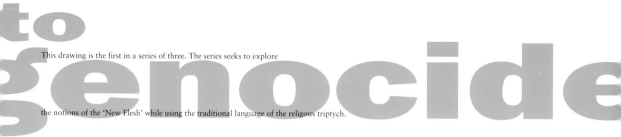

to genocide

This drawing is the first in a series of three. The series seeks to explore the notions of the 'New Flesh' while using the traditional language of the religous triptych.

'New Flesh' is the expression used to describe the changes that technology inflicts on the body. Technologies

expand our limited bodily dexterity, allowing us to perceive and manipulate matter on a scale far larger or

same self, distributed in different sectors of the cyborgian spacescape. It is also foreseeable that these entities could eventually become amalgamations of virtual and vital intelligences. This potential for intelligence melding has been explored in many fictional scenarios – for example, in 'real' space, by the Borg of *Star Trek: The Next Generation*: 'The Borg travel though the reaches of far space in their/its space cube habitat, searching for consumables ... The ship appears a maze of machines where the humanoid Borg components plug themselves in ...' But there is a 'confusion about whether the Borg is a single functioning unit or made up of separate parts – an "it" or a "they"'.4 We will no doubt draw heavily on science-fiction narratives, where such visceral escapology has been examined frequently and extensively. The virtual persona of the cyborg is complex and difficult to define since its capacities and relationship to its fleshed self are fluctuating and varied. The virtual world is one of anthropocentric invisibility, of consensual hallucination, of artificial life and artificial intelligence, of aliases, copies and versions, of mental uploading. It is a domain of ecstatic emergences, flowering and mating genetic algorithms, self-replication, hyperstructures and recursion. These are the prima materia of its architectures.

While the cyberspatial cyborg can be the progeny of its fleshed partner (both offspring and lover), the virtual cyborg does not necessarily have to have a monogamous relationship with a fleshed, wet spouse. The virtual sustainability of 'unreal' lifeforms need not be linked to some sort of 'feeder' umbilical cord which traverses the blurred boundary between virtual, vital and viral. These lifeforms can become self-deter-

smaller than we could naturally.

This first piece depicts the 'Hell' of

4 L H Schneekloth, 'Notions of the Inhabited', in *Ordering Space – Types in Architecture and Design*, eds. K A Franck and L H Schneekloth, Van Nostrand Reinhold, New York, 1994, p. 47.

our contemporary

existence on an

inert, polluted planet, in

fear of bodily decay

and, finally,

death.

5 G Egan, *Permutation City*, Millennium, London, 1995, p. 5.

mining; we can play God and give them free will. In his book *Permutation City*,5 Greg Egan explores many of the familiar notions of the role and nature of the cyberspatial cyborg within a fairly straightforward survival plot which revolves around a series of software personality copies. Each copy is a version of someone still alive (in real terms and time) or someone dead, or a copy of a copy. Each software configuration then develops independently of its original, creating versions with shared and part-shared familial memory. These characters are all part of the life and construction of a new virtual world, a place of refuge from the terrors of software erasure, be it by sabotage or mistake. The fear of erasure takes over from the fear of death. Egan makes us realise that the lot of a copy might not be all it is cracked up to be, not all immortality and roses. 'People reacted badly to waking up as Copies. Paul knew the statistics. Ninety-eight per cent of Copies made were of the very old or the terminally ill. People for whom it was the last resort – most of whom had spent millions beforehand, exhausting all the traditional medical options; some of whom had even died between the taking of the scan and the time the Copy itself was run. Despite this, fifteen per cent decided on awakening – usually in a matter of hours – that they couldn't face living this way.'

Egan calls the up- or downloading of consciousness or the software copying of wet neural networks into cyberspace, 'scanning'; whereas Hans Moravec, a scientist specialising in robotics, has a much more invasive process in mind to achieve this aim: 'A futuristic robot surgeon peels away the brain of a conscious patient, using sensors to analyse and simulate the function in every slice … Eventually your skull is empty, and the surgeon's hand rests deep in your brainstem. Though

digital dreams

you haven't lost consciousness, your mind has been removed from the brain and transferred to a machine.'[6]

6 C Platt, 'Super Humanism', interview with Hans Moravec in *Wired*, October 1995.

In Egan's world order, other cyberspatial cyborgian entities include various software gophers and daemons acting out relatively complex tasks: siphoning mail, sorting information and working creatively to explore new ideas and databases in order to educate themselves and their fleshed counterparts. Egan's narrative also features 'the Lambertians', purely software-evolved insect-like intelligences whose virtual world is Autoverse, Egan's alternative copy environment, a hidden software Utopia/Valhalla. He recognises that evolutionary procedures and their genetic algorithmic programmes are already hugely important in the continuing researches into artificial life and artificial intelligence. A Lambertian puts food under its wings in an external wet sack and is described thus: 'It was no insect by the terrestrial definition; there were four legs, not six, and the body was clearly divided into five segments: the head; sections bearing the forelegs, wings and hind legs; and the tail ... The head was blunt, not quite flat, with two large eyes – if they were eyes, shiny bluish discs, with no apparent structure. The rest of the head was coated in fine hairs, lined up in a complex, symmetrical pattern which reminded Maria of Maori facial tattoos. Sensors for vibration – or scent?'[7] So we see that in Egan's world the cyberspatial cyborgian may evolve into forms that are alien, fundamentally different from the fleshed cyborg which will remain dependent on wet engineering and gravity for some time yet. Much has been made of the 'Aesthetics of Disappearance',[8] to use Paul Virilio's term. And these observations are made possi-

7 Egan, op. cit. p. 221.

8 P Virilio, *The Aesthetics of Disappearance*, Semiotext(e), New York, 1991.

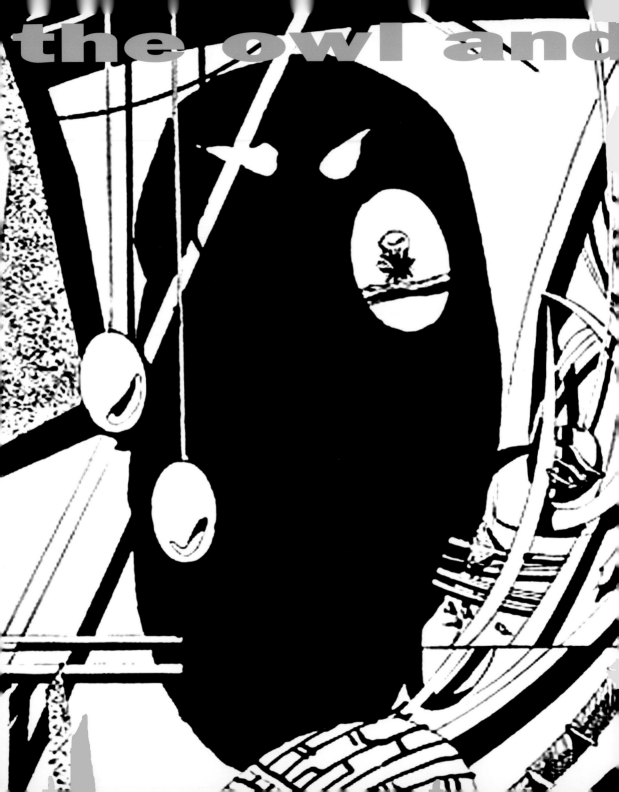

Hieronymus Bosch, the most surreal painter of medieval religous cosmology, used a variety of symbolic techniques to communicate his beliefs. One of his symbols for the Devil was the owl, silently watching over the debauchery of the world. It has been postulated that Bosch was a Cathar,[1] a member of a religous sect, persecuted by the Inquisition, who believed that the earth was Hell and all matter was the work of the Devil. There are many parallels between Cathar beliefs and the proponents of the 'New Flesh'.

[1] The theory that Bosch was a Cathar is excellently framed in Lynda Harris' *The Secret Heresy of Hieronymus Bosch*, Floris Books, 1995.

ble by the availability, ease of transmission and 'lightness' of information, and the ability swiftly to restructure and recalculate modifications in the virtual worlds. These kinds of disappearance have also had an impact on the wetware world of the body, with applications such as nanotechnology (which claims to be able to manipulate material atom by atom) making death and ageing a mere menu option. Deleuze and Guattari have written of the Body without Organs (BwO) but, as Scott Bukatman puts it: 'BwO is opposed not to the organs but the organisation of the organism.'[9] One is not (not here, anyway) arguing for a disappeared, disembodied organism, but for a fleshed, wet intelligence – in effect, a Body with extra Organs (BwxO), where flesh has become even more abundant, hypersensitive and not despised.

[9] S Bukhatmen, *Terminal Identity*, Duke University Press, 1993, p. 328.

You Thing Rike Jelly Fish Pretty Soon[10]

Let us return to the fleshed body, the realspatial cyborg, and consider the technologies of genetics and other bioengineering procedures of the future that will allow it to continue its existence and flourish. Already, even at their genesis, these technologies are able to rectify some aspects of the defective rubbish of the born body. Currently, the gene-therapied or bioengineered body looks no different to us, but it will not always be so. These changes to the body will affect the way we calibrate the universe. But what happens when the ruler stretches, morphs, liquifies and disappears, or when it is here and there simultaneously? As Manly P Hall makes us aware: 'The religious world of today is almost totally ignorant of the fact that the science of biology is the fountainhead of its doctrines and tenets. Many of the codes

[10] W Burroughs, quoted in *Mondo 2000 – A User's Guide to the New Edge*, 1992.

The Ship of Fools, another of Bosch's symbols, is the place where 'souls succumb to the temptations of the world'. Our ship is perched on top of the holey globe, manned by fools who understand little of the inability of their spiked and heavy stone craft to float and glide in the ether of cybernetic connectedness.

and laws believed by modern divines to have been direct revelations from Divinity are in reality the fruitage of ages of patient delving into the intricacies of the human constitution and the infinite wonders revealed by such a study.'[11] As the body changes, so will religion, as we shall see.

11 M P Hall, *The Secret Teachings of All Ages*, The Philosophical Society Inc., Los Angeles, 1988.

But let us first examine one aspect of the liberating and potentially devastating technology of nano engineering. Nano holds the key to the alchemic transmutation of matter, a potential that – should it be fully achievable – will consolidate its incredible influence not only on the inert and concrete but on the body itself. One of nano's more outrageous claims is that a type of telepathy exists between organisms. Here I quote Eric Drexler: 'Authors have written of the direct sharing of thoughts and emotions from mind to mind. Nanotechnology seems likely to make possible some form of this by linking neural structures via transducers and electromagnetic signals. Though limited to the speed of light, this sort of telepathy seems as possible as telephony.'[12] So the fleshed cyborg will be telepathic, probably across a variety of scales, with a much enhanced awareness of itself and 'others'.

12 K E Drexler, *Engines of Creation*, p. 234.

Once perfected, a technology such as genetic engineering will encourage a concept of genetic cross-pollination between species. Eugenically engineered hybrids could be created to establish organisms with a maximised sensitiveness gleaned from a variety of disparate organic and non-organic sources. This theme has been picked up by the author Jeff Noon in his novel *Pollen*.[13] Set in a Manchester of the near future, its characters are Dogmen, Dogbitches, Robodogs, Shadows, Zombies and other genetic hybrids, all

13 J Noon, *Pollen*, Ringpull Press Ltd, London, 1995.

ripped and torn

In Bosch's *The Garden of Earthly Delight*, Satan is represented as a 'Hollow Monster'. The pleasures of the world have become torments. The 'hollow monster' supports the whole composition, yet is also pierced by it. Here the Devil is the body, its flesh cage impaled on the sharp scalpels of technology.

prone to the 'Vurt', a feather-induced drug that is inhaled or swallowed. Mr Noon has a great imagination and has much fun with us, as in the following extract: 'She was a young woman, almost out of college, studying bio-plastics and Hardwere, those twin foundations of robotic canine life. Christina was genetically perfect, with a crystal clear intelligence and her tutors at the University of Manchester had praised the "objective" eye she had brought to her studies of metadogology.' In *Pollen*, hybrids are bred during a great fecundity; in our real world it seems we are now on the verge of a real fecundity, the flesh fecundity. Other authors such as Vernor Vinge have expressed a similar view. 'When a race succeeds in making creatures that are smarter than it is then all the rules change. And from the standpoint of that race, you've gone through a singularity ... Their Art would not be art that you or I at this time could understand.'[14] Or, to paraphrase, their architecture would not be understandable to us at this time.

14 V Vinge, *Mondo 2000 – A User's Guide to the New Edge*, 1992.

Perhaps the William Burroughs quote in the above heading should be seen as a call to arms, or a call to flesh – not a hymn to disappearance but a psalm to fleshiness. Our bodily destiny is, perhaps, not to escape or to trash the flesh cage but to pad it with additional permeable and sensitive flesh. This hyperfleshiness, augmented by the amplified advantages of our distributed virtual agents and selves, is one of our potential evolutionary destinies. Much cyberliterature has been perplexed by the limitation of current virtual-reality soft- and hardware, where full bodily immersion in cyberspace involves a hellish world of experiential inertia and clunky prosthetics. The use of hypersensitised flesh could well provide an alternative to the tyranny of datasuits and head-mounted displays.

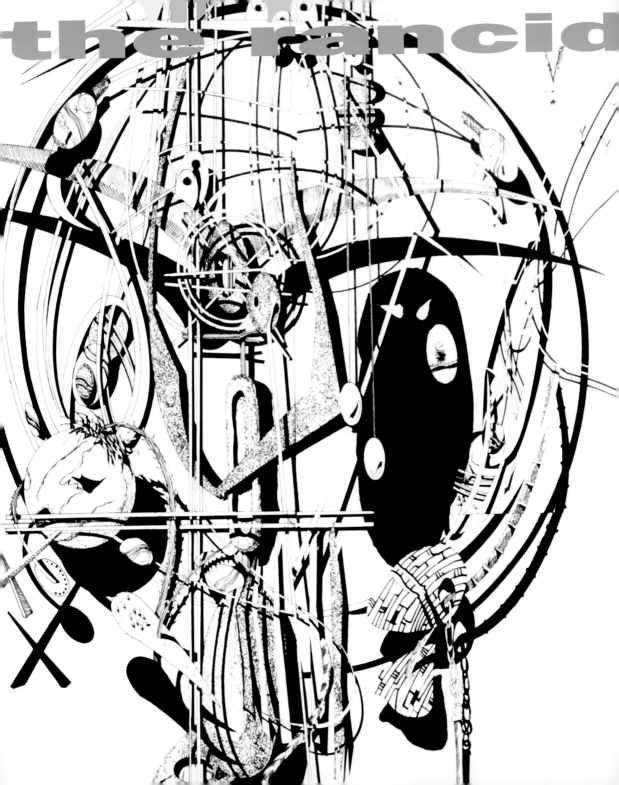

Currently our tombs are layers; the body and the world are but two. Our globe is a polluted orb, and Satan's owl glares from within it.

We are perhaps closer than we think to making visually manifest what is already in existence – our cybernetised metaconsciousness – by means of the flow of information at ever-increasing bit speed through a globally networked series of flesh components. Greg Bear's novel *Blood Music*[15] explores some of these notions of networked intelligence and the role of the subsumed individual within such a structure. 'Bernard had lost his human form in the early morning. The cameras had recorded the transformation. Now, a grey and brown mass lay on his bed, portions extending to the floor on two sides. The mass moved fitfully, sometimes experiencing a short, violent shudder.' It is possible that such smart, biological structures might evolve, complemented by cyberspaces. These cyberspaces might be contained not in silicon hardware but in the biocomputable microbes, bacteria and enzymes of the secretions and cell structures of the new flesh. We return to Bear's narrative: 'I can go off in a million directions, lead a million lives (and not just in the "blood music"– in a universe of Thought, Imagination, Fantasy!) and then gather my selves together, hold a conference and start all over again. Narcissism beyond pride, propinquitous, far grander than simply living forever …'[16]

15 G Bear, *Blood Music*, Legend, 1985, p. 237.

The Stone Christ is Hiding

Orlan, the performance artist mentioned earlier, questions our bodily compliance with Nature and the genetic programme. She considers her work blasphemous. She subjects herself to a series of operations/performances that readjust her face, through the Euphrenic[17] process of surgery. Her work is confirmation that humankind now has dominion over the flesh. For one of Orlan's future

16 Bear, ibid. p. 239.

17 Armstrong, op. cit. In human biology, Euphrenic processes are those that involve unnatural surgical intervention.

corrupt

seed

The symbolism of the seed, fruit and grain symbolises Incarnation, Satan's way of trapping the 'soul' in the matter of a sick and inert world.

performances, she aims to have the largest nose her lungs and facial structure can sustain. The successful completion of this performance will be dependent on a series of bone- and skin-stretching preliminaries.

What we are witnessing here are the death throes of the western God. Until now humankind has invested omnipotence and divine knowledge in the Deity, and has been willing to trust in His judgement at times of various occurrences, particularly ageing, debilitating accidents and the moment of death. As we have seen, the cyberspatial half of the cyborg has already been liberated – and immortality, serial and parallel selves, resurrection, evolution and omnipotence are all within its programming. In his book *The Metaphysics of Virtual Reality*,[18] Michael Heim describes this human craving for omniscience: 'What better way, then, to emulate God's Knowledge than to generate a virtual world constituted by bits of information? To such a cyberworld human beings could enjoy a God-like instant access.' The digital bit is immortal, instantly redefinable, and easily reproduced. So, in the ether of cyberspace the cyber-cyborg's future is assured. But what of the fleshed cyborg when, out here in the 'real' world, it again craves the God-like status of omnipresence, immortality and resurrection? Could our technologies – such as biotechnology, nanotechnology and other Euphrenic processes – liberate us sufficiently to join the realm of the gods, as we virtually can in cyberspace? Michael Heim also refers to the Russian, Nikolai Fedorovich Fedorov, who in the latter half of the nineteenth century believed that the domination of Nature by technology was the ultimate altruistic goal, and that the resurrection of our ancestors was the fundamental altruistic gesture. 'According to Christian

18 M Heim, *The Metaphysics of Virtual Reality*, Oxford University Press, 1993.

belief the dead will rise again so that Christ, in a final judgement, will reorganise and completely redeem the world. The
bodies of all human beings will one day rise again, and this
resurrection will take place through the work of human beings
who carry out the divine plan. The long-range goal of human
co-operation must be to discover the laws of Nature to such a
depth that we can eventually reconstitute the bodies of past
human beings from their remaining physical parti-

19 Heim, ibid. p. 120.   cles still floating about in the universe.'[19] From
this stance we can perceive echoes of Greg Bear's omnipresent
Oneness of *Blood Music*.

Although Fedorov's vision seems off-beat, we have the
theoretical ability to go far beyond it. We may have the ability
to animate not just past lifeforms but also previously inanimate forms. Hall gives us a spiritual view: 'When humanity
has completed its physical evolution, the empty shell of materiality left behind will be used by other *life waves* [my italics]
as stepping stones to their own liberation.'[20] Again

20 Hall, op. cit.   we look to Greg Bear, and his short story 'Petra',
for inspiration: 'They saw the stone ornaments of the Cathedral come alive. With someone to see and believe, in a universe lacking another foundation, my ancestors shook off
stone and became flesh. Centuries of rock celibacy

21 G Bear, 'Petra' in   weighed upon them.'[21] The Stone Christ had gone
Mirrorshades, ed. Bruce   missing from the Cathedral, but was in fact hiding
Stirling, Paladin, 1988.   in one of its dark recesses. The teller of the story
encounters Him. 'I'd have to come from their midst, anony-
mous and that is clearly impossible. No, leave them alone for
a while. They'll make Me over again, perhaps, or better still,
forget about Me. About us. We don't have any

22 Bear, ibid.   place there.'[22]

Hans Moravec perceives the future as the domain of miniaturised machines, with humanity as a pampered menagerie illustrating the machines' evolutionary history. This is a future of supersmart, robotised intelligences, not of a fleshed fecundity. He also has a vision of God: 'And Moravec's vision of a supremely powerful artificial intelligence that will love humanity enough to re-create it is basically a vision of God – the only difference being that in his scheme of things, we create God version 1.0, after which it builds its own enhancements.'[23] Interestingly, the issue that gave Fedorov the moral and philosophical base for his promotion of the benefits of science and technology appears also in one of Moravec's scenarios. 'Assuming the artificial intelligences now have truly overwhelming processing power, they should be able to reconstruct human society in every detail by tracing atomic events backwards in time … It will cost them very little to preserve us this way … They will in fact, be able to re-create a model of our entire civilisation, with everything and everyone in it, down to the atomic level, simulating our atoms with machinery which is largely sub-atomic.'[24] Arguably, this event could have already taken place, but how can we know one way or the other? Resurrection may have already occurred. While we are killing the One God, we are pushing ourselves into a God-like role, in a future where we take on the Deity's mantle and become the Many Gods. Humankind has taken on the job of both Christ and God. We know that Godliness is next to wetness as well as bittyness. The Christ of architecture, the body, has influenced architecture since humankind first sheltered from the rain and predators. It is now hiding, unsure whether it will need architecture again. The architecture of the future will be

23 Platt, op. cit.

24 Platt, op. cit.

homogeneous, networked, highly sensitised, telepathic, moist, dry, digital and biological. Few of today's architectural tactics will be of any use in these central yet peripheral locations in the spacescape. Vernor Vinge's Singularity may well be on its way, and architecture may be torn apart.

the new wet satanic mills

Human kind cannot bear very much reality.
  T S Eliot

The Luddite philosophies of some environmental and ecological organisations have a superficial resonance when one surveys such ecological problems as the depletion of the ozone layer, crude oil washing over our coastlines, polluted air, acid rain and the like. The source of these contemporary apocalyptic conditions is easy to identify in a world where the dominance and influence of technology and its machines extend throughout all of contemporary culture.

The sentiment expressed by E O Wilson – that 'Luddites and anti-intellectuals do not master the differential equations of thermodynamics or the biochemical cures for illness. They stay in thatched huts and die young' – reminds us that machines are designed, developed and sold because they are manifestations of desires that our slushy viscera cannot deliver unaided. It is clear that at the moment we are killing ourselves to live. Nevertheless, the resultant demonising of advanced technology and its benefits and bodily invasions is a short-sighted response. Humankind is stupid, selfish, greedy and murderously dangerous, yet simultaneously capable of considerable compassion, gentleness, creativity and good sense. This is the human condition, paradoxical though it may be. To cast technology as one of humanity's great follies is misguided. The romantic notion that the world was once, and will one day return to, an arcadian Utopia for rosy-cheeked, self-sufficient folk who smell of wood smoke, make dresses and wardrobes, and grow vegetables, is erroneous. This fantasy/solution stinks of guilt, (self)denial and medieval fortitude. It is a manifestation of the inherent dualism in the human psyche, of the constant battle between mechanistic and vitalist views of the world. The spectre of technology is represented by the generic myths of Dracula and Frankenstein; the history of such stories illustrates just how deep-rooted they are in our psyche, and our fear that after our exile from Eden our creations have been somewhat flawed – even cruelly dangerous.

It is indeed frightening when one learns that 50 per cent of Americans do not believe in evolution. Ignorance, fear and short-sighted religious piety still confuse our conception of progress. Our only hope for continuing the evolution of the fleshed cyborg (for that is what we have become) is to embrace the future benefits of our technologies, surreal as they may at first seem. While it is true that our current bulk technologies have rented the delicate hyperstructural management of our ecosystem, in the future it is likely that, given current developments in molecular technologies, we will be able to produce many hybrid or natural materials that are biodegradable. The future may not be about dirty mass-production processes; instead there may be vats of bacteria where the production of materials is induced as part of a doctored, natural digestive cycle. In this way it may be possible to produce cell energy stores for use by human beings. Once the manufacture of biologically produced materials on a sizeable scale becomes a reality, the huge potential of some of nature's more incredible proteins and materials – including elastin (the material of the lungs), keratin (the carapace of insects) and spider silk with its amazing strength-to-weight ratio – will be liberated. These products – and many others – can potentially be produced by judicial gene splicing; that is, by introducing artificial genes into bacterial DNA. These genes will then encourage the bacteria to produce proteins that are either naturally produced or purely artificial. The ecological benefits of this technology are obvious once it is considered that the bacteria populate water at around body temperature and consume nat-

digital dreams

ural amino acids. Therefore, internal conditions of any manufacturing facility containing these cultures must, prima facie,
support life and thus be 'green'. In genetic research the species
constantly used is the common fruit fly, and in bacteria
research it is *E. coli*, the common gut bacteria. During 1990,
E. coli was conditioned to produce an artificial silk-like protein. Among other breakthroughs that it is reasonable to
expect is the development of fibronectin, a protein that sticks
cells together in the body; this will aid the compatibility of
natural and artificially cultured tissue and will therefore be
useful in many wound repair and surgical procedures. Flesh is
already being cultured on biodegradable 'scaffolding'.
Researches indicate that the creation of a whole arm is theoretically possible. Initially, few designers will sculpt objects in
flesh, but as time goes by this skill will become more common.

It seems that once this technology comes fully on line,
architects and designers of all sorts will have a greatly
increased palette of materials with which to design. For example, materials with properties similar to spider silk could be
used in vehicular products and architectural and fashion
design, where protective strength and resilience under pressure
are primary considerations. Another avenue to explore could
be the provision of bioreactors and biosensors, where the pro-
tein-producing function is controlled and activated by light,
electricity, or some other phenomenon. Such technology is yet
another example of how the synthesised is hybridising with
the natural, creating both new materials and new paradigms
of interactivity that do not damage the earth's sensitive ecological balance.

But the advantages of looking at material production in
this way go even further. It is not unreasonable to assume that

bacteria could be 'doped' and used to start the decontamination of areas polluted by bulk manufacture. This would be done by doctoring bacterial genes in such a way as to encourage them to feed on previously unclearable molecular detritus, breaking it down into reusable or harmless byproducts. New materials with keratin-like qualities also offer exciting possibilities. Keratin is a major constituent of insect physiology (its plastic yet strong qualities enable claws and pupae to harden slowly in the sun and air). Architects and product designers have a long history of trying to mimic certain aspects of insect morphology; in the future it will be far easier for them to do so successfully.

Technology is at a cathartic moment: its relationship to the natural world is on the verge of becoming less parasitic and more symbiotic. As mentioned earlier, technology is critical to the continued existence of our cyborgian bodies. But we must remember that many of us need numerous drugs and devices to maintain the status quo of our personal existence, whether they be asthma inhalers, the 4000 drugs in a cigarette, or cars and aeroplanes. Gene therapies are becoming more common for a variety of ailments – and are initial steps towards recoding our genetic inheritance. Obviously, there are still a number of ethical problems to be debated and overcome. But in exchange for the promise of freedom from the tyranny of familial illness, or of liberation from a fault of the body's architecture, is it not worth confronting some of our most illogical notions of the body's integrity?

In the light of these and other technological aspirations, it seems short-sighted to continue to suggest that high technology is a danger to our eco system. Bertolt Brecht's view that the role of science is 'not to open the door to everlasting wis-

　　　　　　　　　　　digital dreams

dom but to set the limit on everlasting error', seems appropriate. The future for designers does not have to be conditioned by a 'back-to-basics' puritanism and inert, natural, handcrafted, slow and labour-intensive manufacturing processes. Designers will have to consider the efficacy of their design decisions and priorities in relation not only to the construction of their objects but to the use of these objects in an ecology of reuse and bioreconfiguration. We must have the courage to embrace the concept of technological progress – and to see science as the hero, not the villain.

index

10

11

12-13

20

21

26
29

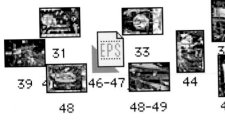
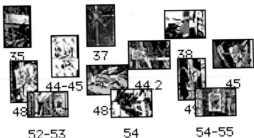

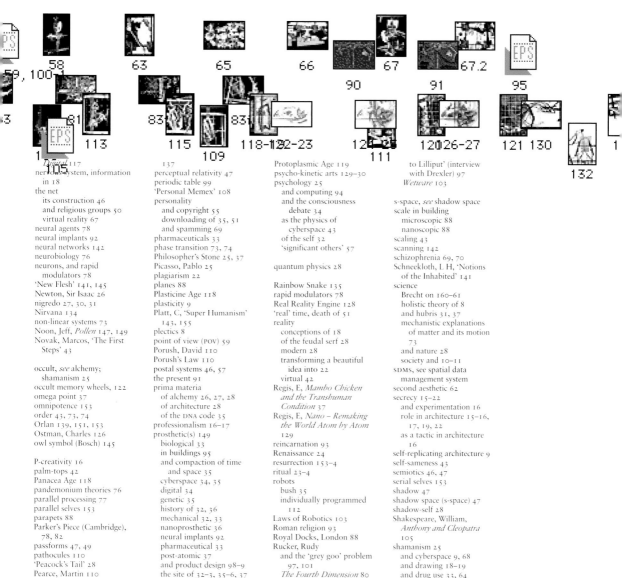

33   134–135   136   50, 152   137

digital dreams